Rain Forests

Rain Forests

Other books in the At Issue series:

At ✳ Issue

Rain Forests

Stuart A. Kallen, *Book Editor*

Bruce Glassman, *Vice President*
Bonnie Szumski, *Publisher*
Helen Cothran, *Managing Editor*

GREENHAVEN PRESS
An imprint of Thomson Gale, a part of The Thomson Corporation

THOMSON
™
GALE

Detroit • New York • San Francisco • San Diego • New Haven, Conn.
Waterville, Maine • London • Munich

LIBRARY OF CONGRESS CATALOGING-IN-PUBLICATION DATA

Rain forests / Stuart A. Kallen, book editor.
    p. cm. — (At issue)
Includes bibliographical references and index.
ISBN 0-7377-2741-1 (lib. : alk. paper) — ISBN 0-7377-2742-X (pbk. : alk. paper)
    1. Rain forest ecology. 2. Rain forest conservation. I. Kallen, Stuart A., 1955– .
II. At issue (San Diego, Calif.)
QH541.5.R27R355 2006
333.75'16—dc22   2005047196

Contents

Introduction

Rain forests take up only about 6 percent of the earth's landmass but their importance to the environment transcends their geographical boundaries. Drenched with 160 to 400 inches of rain annually, tropical forests contain over half the plant and animal species on Earth. The forest vegetation removes carbon dioxide, or CO_2, from the atmosphere and slows the effects of global warming. In addition, rain forests are home to millions of indigenous people who depend on the resources of the environment to support their traditional cultures. These valuable natural resources include petroleum, natural gas, rare minerals, medicinal plants, and hardwood trees such as teak and mahogany.

Who should control these resources—or whether they should be developed at all—is a matter of contentious debate between environmentalists, scientists, government officials, indigenous people, and business interests. Thomas P. Tomich, the principal economist and global coordinator for the Alternatives to Slash-and-Burn Programme, a sustainable agriculture organization, explains the conflict over rain forests:

> Everyone in the world wants something from tropical forests. . . . Forest dwellers wish to continue a way of life they've known for generations. They are losing their land to migrant [farmers], who clear small amounts of forest to earn a living by raising crops and livestock. Both these groups tend to lose out to larger, more powerful interests—ranchers, plantation owners, large-scale farmers or logging concerns—whose aim is to convert large areas of forest into big money. Outside the forests is the international community, who wish to see forests preserved for the biodiversity they harbour.

The conflicts discussed by Tomich are clearly illustrated by the case of Venezuela, a nation that contains approximately 151,000 square miles of largely undisturbed old-growth rain forest. Venezuelan rain forests are among the most diverse in the world, with an estimated fifteen thousand types of plant species. The forests also contain diamonds, bauxite, iron ore, 11 percent of the world's supply of gold, and a reserve of crude oil worth billions of dollars. Despite this natural wealth, 80 percent of Venezuela's 23 million citizens are mired in poverty. While government and business interests are working to develop the resources of the rain forest and improve the economy, environmentalists say their actions are causing serious damage to the land.

In the remote southern Venezuelan state of Amazonas, gold miners practice extremely destructive gold mining techniques. They uproot trees with hydraulic water pumps that wash away the thin layers of soil to reveal the gold beneath the ground. Mercury, used to purify the gold, pours into waterways and poisons rare and exotic fish and bird species. The influx of miners is also destroying the traditional lifestyles of the indigenous Yanomami people. Miners have evicted the Yanomami from their ancestral lands while inadvertently infecting them with deadly diseases such as smallpox, to which the tribes have little natural resistance.

The rain forests of eastern Venezuela are also impacted by mining. These lands contain valuable bauxite, a mineral used to produce aluminum for beverage cans, automobiles, airplanes, and other products. This mineral is mined in the forests and shipped to sprawling aluminum factories located in Ciudad Guayana, situated on the Orinoco River. The industrialized nature of the city is described by journalist Donovan Webster in the *National Geographic* magazine:

> The Orinoco [River] is fouled by floating garbage, downed trees, and technicolor spills that shimmy, amoebae-like, with oil. . . . Along the shore a string of yellow railcars, carrying 90 tons of ore apiece, rolls downriver from Cerro Bolivar, the iron-rich mountain 75 miles away. At the wharves the ore is dumped . . . into crushers. . . . The Orinoco, once chest deep and home to a few Yanomami, has grown into a global main street.

Although the factories of Ciudad Guayana have polluted the rain forest, they have also provided jobs for thousands of poor Venezuelans.

The conflict between environmental preservation and human need seen in Venezuela is representative of controversies in other rain forest nations in South America, Asia, Africa, and elsewhere. In most of these areas, the population has more than doubled since 1950. To support this growing population, the rain forests have been destroyed to provide food, fuel, and other natural resources for local inhabitants. Other rain forest resources are sold to industrial nations to bolster the local economies. According to the National Academy of Sciences, at least 50 million acres of rain forest are lost annually worldwide, an area the size of Great Britain. In Venezuela alone, 41 percent of the original rain forest has been destroyed, and 40 percent of the remaining forest is threatened.

The question of how best to preserve the rain forests while providing for human needs will not be easily solved. While some wish to protect the lands in their natural state to save endangered species and ward off global warming, others seek to utilize the rain forests' resources for more immediate needs. Unless the conflict between economics and the environment is resolved, the future of the planet's oldest forests is at great risk.

1

The Destruction of the Amazon Rain Forest Is Polluting the World's Atmosphere

Henry Chu

Henry Chu is a staff writer for the Los Angeles Times.

For decades environmentalists have said that the Amazon rain forest is the "lungs of the world" because it produces oxygen while consuming carbon dioxide, a gas that contributes to global warming. Unfortunately, the forest is being destroyed by fires set by farmers, loggers, and ranchers. As the rain forest burns, carbon dioxide is released into the atmosphere, polluting the air and accelerating global warming. Until the Brazilian government can summon the willpower to stop this destruction, the burning of the Amazon rain forest will continue to harm the various climates of the world.

The death of a myth begins with stinging eyes and heaving chests here on the edge of the Amazon rain forest.

Every year, fire envelops the jungle, throwing up inky billows of smoke that blot out the sun. Animals flee. Residents for miles around cry and wheeze, while the weak and unlucky develop serious respiratory problems.

When the burning season strikes, life and health in the Amazon falter, and color drains out of the riotous green landscape as great swaths of majestic trees, creeping vines, delicate bromeliads and hardy ferns are reduced to blackened stubble.

But more than just the land, these annual blazes also lay waste to a cherished notion that has roosted in the popular mind for decades: the idea of the rain forest as the "lungs of the world."

Ever since saving the Amazon became a fashionable cause in the 1980s, championed by Madonna, Sting and other celebrities, the jungle has consistently been likened to an enormous recycling plant that slurps up carbon dioxide and pumps out oxygen for us all to breathe, from Los Angeles to London to Lusaka.

Think again, scientists say.

Far from cleaning up the atmosphere, the Amazon is now a major source for pollution. Rampant burning and deforestation, mostly at the hands of illegal loggers and of ranchers, release hundreds of millions of tons of carbon dioxide into the skies each year.

> *Rampant burning and deforestation, mostly at the hands of illegal loggers and of ranchers, release hundreds of millions of tons of carbon dioxide into the skies each year.*

Brazil now ranks as one of the world's leading producers of greenhouse gases, thanks in large part to the Amazon, the source for up to two-thirds of the country's emissions.

"It's not the lungs of the world," said Daniel Nepstad, an American ecologist who has studied the Amazon for 20 years. "It's probably burning up more oxygen now than it's producing."

Scientists such as Nepstad prefer to think of the world's largest tropical rain forest as Earth's air conditioner. The region's humidity, they say, is vital in climate regulation and cooling patterns in South America—and perhaps as far away as Europe.

The Amazon's role as a source of pollution, not a remover of it, is directly linked to the galloping rate of destruction in the region over the last quarter-century.

The dense and steamy habitat straddles eight countries and

is home to up to 20% of the world's fresh water and 30% of its plant and animal species.

Brazil's portion accounts for more than half the entire eco-system. Official figures show that, on average, 7,500 square miles of rain forest were chopped and burned down in Brazil every year between 1979 and 2004. Over the 25 years, it's as if a forest the size of California had disappeared from the face of the Earth.

Such encroachment on virgin land is theoretically illegal or subject to tough regulation, but the government here lacks the resources—some say, the will—to enforce environmental protection laws.

Loggers, Ranchers, and Farmers

Loggers are typically the first to punch through, hacking crude roads and harvesting all the precious hardwoods they can find. One gang of woodcutters, in cahoots with crooked environmental-protection officials, cut down nearly $371 million worth of timber from 1990 until it was busted in the biggest sting operation of its kind in Brazil, authorities said last week [June 2005].

Close on the loggers' heels are big ranchers and farmers, who torch the remaining vegetation to clear the way for cattle and crops such as soy, Brazil's new star export, which is claiming ever larger quantities of land.

> *Brazil and other poor countries are not required to reduce their emissions of greenhouse gases.*

Prime burning period in the Amazon runs from July to January, the dry season. In 2004, government satellite images of the forest registered 165,440 "hot spots," fires whose flames can shoot as high as 100 feet and push temperatures beyond 2,500 degrees.

These tremendous blazes spew about 200 million tons of carbon emissions into the atmosphere each year, which translates into several times that amount in actual carbon dioxide. In contrast, Brazil's consumption of fossil fuels, the chief source of greenhouse gases worldwide, creates less than half what the fires send up.

During burning season, dark palls of smoke settle over parts of the jungle for days.

"It becomes hard to see, and your eyes have problems. The kids all get sick and have trouble breathing," said Joaquim Borges da Silva, 42, a rural worker who lives in a small encampment here in Remanso Talisma, on the forest's outskirts.

> **"** *A shift in climate [in Brazil] could cause a ripple effect, disrupting weather patterns in Antarctica, the Eastern U.S. and even Western Europe.* **"**

Smoke grew so thick at one point last year [2004] that two cars on the road into the camp barreled into each other head-on, killing two people, Borges da Silva said. The fires also kill the game that workers and small settlers rely on for food.

He pointed out a charred tract of land, littered with slumps and felled trees that looked like so many toothpicks, where tractors working 24 hours a day for a month cleared 1,000 acres last year. Trucks rumbled in and out, loaded down with mahogany and cedar.

Farmers subsequently burned the area. Two months later, at the first rain, a small plane swooped in and dropped seeds.

Among the Top Polluters

Even with the burning of the rain forest, Brazil's annual output of carbon pollutants is tiny compared with that of the U.S., which produces nearly 6 billion tons.

But Brazil's share still vaults it onto the Top 10 list of polluters, ahead of industrialized nations such as Canada and Italy.

However, under the international environmental treaty known as the Kyoto Protocol, Brazil and other poor countries are not required to reduce their emissions of greenhouse gases. Nor does the accord contain financial incentives to encourage nations such as Brazil and Indonesia to rein in the destruction of their tropical forests.

"This is a very sensitive issue in Brazil and among developing countries," said Paulo Moutinho, research coordinator for the Amazon Institute of Environmental Studies. "If you want to include developing countries, especially countries with large areas of tropical forests, in some kind of mechanism to mitigate climate change, you need to compensate deforestation reduction."

The federal government here has begun discussing ways of rewarding states for conserving the jungle, but little has been achieved.

In 2004, Brazil lost an estimated 10,000 square miles of forest, the second-worst year on record. Nearly the same amount was destroyed the year before. Environmentalists had hoped that the 2002 election of President Luiz Inacio Lula da Silva, Brazil's first left- leaning leader, would reverse the tide, not accelerate it.

Critics say that despite repeated promises to protect the Amazon, Lula's government has favored the huge farming interests fueling its destruction in order to keep Brazil's economy growing and to boost his chances of reelection next year [2006].

Dangers to the World's Climates

Even without the massive burning, the popular conception of the Amazon as a giant oxygen factory for the rest of the planet is misguided, scientists say. Left unmolested, the forest does generate enormous amounts of oxygen through photosynthesis, but it consumes most of it itself in the decomposition of organic matter.

Researchers are trying to determine what role the Amazon plays in keeping the region cool and relatively moist, which in turn has a hugely beneficial effect on agriculture—ironically, the same interests trying to cut down the forest.

The theory goes that the jungle's humidity, as much as water from the ocean, is instrumental in creating rain over both the Amazon River basin and other parts of South America, particularly western and southern Brazil, where much of this country's agricultural production is concentrated.

"If you took away the Amazon, you'd take away half of the rain that falls on Brazil," Moutinho said. "You can imagine the problems that would ensue."

A shift in climate here could cause a ripple effect, disrupting weather patterns in Antarctica, the Eastern U.S. and even Western Europe, some scholars believe.

This is what worries ecologists about the continued destruction of the rain forest: not the supposed effect on the global air supply, but rather on the weather.

"Concern about the environmental aspects of deforestation now is more over climate rather than [carbon emissions] or whether the Amazon is the 'lungs of the world,'" said Paulo, Barreto, a researcher with the Amazon Institute of People and Environment.

"For sure, the Amazon is not the lungs of the world," he added. "It never was."

2

Claims That Rain Forests Are Being Destroyed Are Exaggerated

David Rothbard and Craig Rucker

David Rothbard and Craig Rucker are president and executive director, respectively, of the Committee for a Constructive Tomorrow (CFACT), an organization they cofounded in 1985 to provide conservative alternatives to major environmental groups like Greenpeace, the Sierra Club, and Friends of the Earth.

Environmentalists often exaggerate statistics when they talk about deforestation in the Amazon rain forest. They routinely claim that anywhere from 27 million to 78 million acres of tropical forests are being destroyed annually. However, careful estimates show that the true figure is closer to 7 million acres per year. Environmentalists also greatly overstate the number of species facing extinction because of rain forest destruction. While indiscriminate destruction of rain forests makes little sense, the people of Brazil, Ecuador, Venezuela, and other Amazonian countries have a right to benefit from the natural resources rain forests provide. However, these developing nations are often prevented from doing so by environmentalists who use inflated figures to predict that rain forests will completely disappear unless they are left untouched.

In the mysterious jungle known as the Amazon, legend had it there lived a Golden King named El Dorado said to be so rich

David Rothbard and Craig Rucker, "Facts Lost in Deep Dark Jungle of Rainforest Issue," www.CFACT.org, January 1, 2003. Copyright © 2003 by CFACT. Reproduced by permission.

that each day he used gold dust to adorn his royal body. For Gonzalo Pizarro, brother of [Francisco Pizarro], the famous conqueror of the Incas, this vision was more than he could bear. So in 1540, setting off with 4,000 Indians, 200 horses, 3,000 swine, and packs of hunting dogs, [Gonzalo] Pizarro breached the Eastern edge of the great jungle and began his quest to find and pillage El Dorado and his land of the cinnamon forests.

Pizarro, of course, never did find the Golden King. And after throwing countless numbers of the hapless tribesmen he came across to the ravenous hounds or roasting them on barbacoa [hot coals] when they denied knowledge of the mythical city, he was forced to return to Quito, Peru a beaten man. He had not found treasure in the Amazon.

Since that time, there have been many others who have descended into the Emerald Forest. But perhaps content with a vision a bit less grandiose, these enterprising souls have found riches abundant in the magnificent natural bounty of this exotic land.

In the Amazon rainforest, some of the richest ore bodies in the world have been discovered. Highly-prized woods such as teak, mahogany, and rosewood can also be found. Over the years, the unique vegetation and growing conditions of the region has produced a virtual pantry of sought-after goods ranging from medicines and spices to a host of distinctively tropical products like rubber, coffee, chocolate, and chewing gum. And this does not even mention the ecological cornucopia hidden beneath the dense green canopy of tropical rainforests which are home to more than two-thirds of the 1.4 million species known to man.

> *The region has produced a virtual pantry of sought-after goods ranging from medicines and spices to a host of distinctively tropical products like rubber, coffee, chocolate, and chewing gum.*

So yes, the Amazon does indeed hold a rich bounty. But it is certainly not the extent of its wealth alone that has recently made the word "rainforest" a common term heard in schoolyards, living rooms, and legislative halls around the world. Rather, it is pictures of the charred remains of once lush jungles and numbers likened to one football field per second that have made the rainforest, and the Amazon in particular, a topic of international concern.

> **❝** *American researchers . . . concluded the average annual rate of [rainforest] loss was just 3.7 million acres, making the global rate just over 7 million, or one-fifth the widely accepted number.* **❞**

Some environmentalists claim that with current rates of destruction, tropical rainforests will all soon be gone, that nearly half the species on planet earth will all soon be extinguished, and that these areas must basically be put off limits to all but a few tribesmen if we are to have any hope of saving what they would call this Eden-like paradise. But in an emotionally-charged issue like the rainforest, getting to the truth can prove almost as hard as finding the glittering city of the ancient Golden King.

The Rate of Rainforest Loss Is Exaggerated

"With the simple ax, the mighty chainsaw, and all-powerful fire . . . each year 28 million acres of tropical forest are destroyed . . . for crop production, fuelwood gathering, and cattle ranching. Commercial timber harvesting degrades at least an additional 11 million." *Sandra Postel, Worldwatch Institute*

So is it 40 million acres per year as Postel suggests? Well that's the number commonly bandied about, but some environmentalists use slightly lower figures. The World Resources Institute says, "Every year, at least 27 million acres of tropical forests are lost—an area the size of Pennsylvania, Ohio, or Virginia." Others say more.

[Former] Vice President Al Gore claims 51 million acres per year are lost. And one of the largest Green groups on this issue, the Rainforest Action Network, says the number is 78 million acres per year, or an area larger than all of Poland.

Where do they get these figures?

It turns out the central basis for the 40 million acres figure comes from a Brazilian scientist who used a U.S. weather satellite to count the number of fires burning in the Amazon at any one time in 1988 (at the height of government-subsidized deforestation), haphazardly guessed at the size of each, and then simply doubled the number to come up with his worldwide total.

However, according to the Heartland Institute, when two American researchers took a more studious look in 1993, painstakingly comparing overhead photos from 1978 and 1988 and entering into a computer every tiny forest clearing, road, and power-line right of way, they concluded the average annual rate of loss was just 3.7 million acres, making the global rate just over 7 million, or one-fifth the widely accepted number.

> *A team of zoologists that combed the Atlantic coastal forests of Brazil could not confirm a single case of extinction, even though those forests have been cut to about 12% of their original size.*

In gridiron terms, this means that if all the world's rainforests equalled one football field, even at the "rapid" destruction rate of the late 1980's (which many experts say won't continue since government subsidies have all but ended and there's currently no way to get into the deeper interior), we would lose less than 3.6 inches per year, and it would take more than 500 years just to make it past midfield.

So it's little wonder that even the usually pessimistic Worldwatch Institute went on the record as saying, "With nearly 90% of its groves still standing . . . the Brazilian Amazon is relatively untouched."

Island Hopping

One cannot paddle his raft very far into a discussion about rainforest loss without talking about the catastrophe this is alleged to be having on the world's species. Environmental biologist Edward O. Wilson claims as many as 50,000 species are being lost each year. . . . But again the question must be asked, where do they get these figures?

[Widely quoted environmentalist Norman] Myers himself

openly admits "we have no way of knowing the actual current rate of extinction in tropical forests, nor can we even make an accurate guess."

So what the alarmed scientists do offer are merely predictions based on a mathematical theory called the "species-area curve." This theory, linked to the study of isolated islands, says that for every 90% loss in area, the number of species that can live there is cut in half. The one little problem with this, though, is that the real world has hardly operated according to the theory.

To state the obvious, islands and continents have enormous differences. While islands are surrounded by water which is usually pretty hostile to land species, terrestrial habitats are surrounded by land, which can accommodate migrating species just a bit more easily.

No doubt this is why only three forest birds went extinct in 300 years in America, even though the virgin woodlands of the eastern U.S. were hacked down to just a fraction of their original area during that time (and for two of the birds, habitat loss didn't even play a major role).

It's also the likely reason a team of zoologists that combed the Atlantic coastal forests of Brazil could not confirm a single case of extinction, even though those forests have been cut to about 12% of their original size.

> *One of the most persistent myths about Amazonia is that it has long been a wilderness, virtually untouched by humans until relatively recently.*

And even on the island of Puerto Rico where human activity reduced the area of primary forest by 99%, the theory didn't hold true since only seven birds became extinct and the total number of species actually increased from 60 at the time of Columbus to 97 today.

The New Iron Curtain

"If people are to have better jobs and make enough money so that they may have better homes and food and clothes, Brazil must develop her resources and expand her Industries. Areas like the Amazon Valley, and much of the interior, must be fully explored." *From the 1961 book, "Let's Visit Brazil"*

Throughout most of the human experience, the idea of developing the natural resources of a land and thereby improving the lives of its people was not even a point of debate. Today, however, instead of looking to a place like the rainforest to see how it can wisely be used to benefit mankind, the prevailing thought is to basically put an iron gate around the whole thing with a big "Keep Out" sign clearly posted.

Most assuredly, the grossly exaggerated numbers concerning deforestation rates and its threat to species have been used to lend credence to this notion. But some advocates have sought to further bolster a "hands-off" agenda by painting the rainforest as an ancient natural paradise, virtually untouched and unspotted by human hands until recent times, and as expressed in one Sierra Club book, as a "fragile, non-renewable resource." Disturb it, they say, and it's simply gone forever.

In reality, according to leading expert Dr. Nigel Smith of the University of Florida, "One of the most persistent myths about Amazonia is that it has long been a wilderness, virtually untouched by humans until relatively recently." He points to evidence showing populations of between one and seven million in Amazonia around A.D. 1500 and concludes, "in spite of the development push that began in the 1960's, it seems unlikely that the area cleared today is any larger than it was in 1500."

Since it's often hard to find even remnants of these lost tribes beneath the thick broad leaves of the Amazonian jungle, the rainforest is apparently more resilient than many would think.

Does this mean we should go in with bulldozers, axes, and fires ablazing? Obviously not. Tropical rainforests are certainly a valuable ecological entity. But just as the U.S. and Europe have been allowed to use significant portions of their land to meet the needs of their people, so too must developing nations like Brazil be given that same opportunity. For in the end, with the environmental conservation that comes with increased wealth, this will likely prove what's best for both man and nature.

3

Oil Production Can Harm Rain Forests

Leslie Jermyn

Leslie Jermyn is a freelance writer and an anthropologist based in Toronto.

In 2003 an oil pipeline that runs through the Amazon rain forest in Ecuador was completed. While multinational corporations working in the Amazon basin reap huge profits from oil production, these companies' industrial practices are causing irreparable damage to the environment. The pipeline does not benefit the majority of Ecuadorians and is a great threat to indigenous people, who are losing the ability to earn even a meager living as the forest they rely on is decimated. Furthermore, the local communities will only receive 0.006 percent of the profits the pipeline generates. The pipeline's developers insist that they followed strict World Bank environmental standards in developing the pipeline; however, a report by a former World Bank employee shows that the developers did not adhere to these standards and did not properly assess the potential damage oil production could cause in the Amazon.

T he city of Lago Agrio [Ecuador] bristled with tension. Protesters had been blocking the streets for two weeks. Ecuador's president declared a state of emergency and sent in military reinforcements to quell the demonstrations. As tempers flared in the glaring sun, helicopters dropped tear gas into the crowds. In the still tropical air, the gas hung close to the

Leslie Jermyn, "Fuelling Disaster: A Controversial Oil Pipeline Now Rips Across Ecuador's Upper Amazon Forests, Damaging What Remains of Ecologically Sensitive Areas and Indigenous Cultures," *This Magazine*, vol. 37, September/October 2003, pp. 12–15. Copyright © 2003 by Red Maple Foundation. Reproduced by permission of the author.

ground. When the fumes finally lifted, two children were dead from asphyxiation. By the time the demonstrators were silenced, two more had been killed and many wounded as a result of clashes with the military.

This February 2002 protest was just one episode in the checkered history of Ecuador's second heavy-crude pipeline, the Oleoducto de Crudos Pesados (OCP). The lead investor in this controversial project is Canadian oil giant EnCana. The Alberta-based company holds the largest stake with 31.4%.

From east to west, oil is physically and politically dividing Ecuador. The pipeline, which stretches from wells in the upper Amazon to refining and shipping facilities on the Pacific coast, was completed this summer [2003] and will pump up to 450,000 barrels of oil per day.

Big business and their financiers argue that Ecuador needs oil revenue to service the country's national debt. But since Texaco struck black gold in the Amazon in 1967, the region has been stripped of forests, covered with pools of black sludge and its Cofan indigenous nation brought to the brink of extinction. Ecuadorians living in oil territory are among the poorest in a poor country, even though the industry produces more than 40% of export earnings. The city of Lago Agrio—"sour lake" in Spanish—has become a bitter symbol of oil development. The city of 23,000 had more than 200 murders last year [2002] and child prostitution is rampant.

Citizen groups, indigenous organizations, environmentalists and expert observers believe more oil development will destroy what remains of upper Amazon forests and indigenous cultures, damage other ecologically sensitive areas and provide no long term development for the country. They are convinced that the pipeline will never benefit the majority of Ecuadorians and no amount of cash will heal the social divisions or environmental wounds it has caused.

Putting the Environment at Risk

When the clouds descend on the ridges of the Mindo Nambillo Cloudforest Reserve, there is an eerie quiet punctuated only by the sound of dripping water and birdsong. The area is home to 450 species of birds, many of which are endemic and endangered. Locals depend on this diversity to attract ecotourists, their primary source of income.

Edwin, an indigenous nature guide, is passionate about this

landscape and loves his job guiding visitors through it. Along with tourists and other guides, Edwin was part of a tree-camp protest aimed at blocking pipeline construction. Their protest lasted three months, until the Ecuadorian government arrested 17 tree sitters in March 2002.

"They chose this route to avoid building another pumping station to get the oil over the mountains," Edwin says. "This pipeline puts the reserve, the birds and our water source at risk." Thanks to OCP, a seven-metre-wide swath of exposed earth now slices through the forest, climbing steep hills and cutting off the tops of ridges to make room for the buried pipe.

The OCP denies charges that they took the northern route to save costs. The consortium's Environmental Impact Assessment is a nine-volume document that justifies the northern route. "We looked at different routes and decided that this is the best one," says Ray Kohut, director of environment and community relations at OCP. "We, as a company, are following World Bank guidelines."

> *Since Texaco struck black gold in the Amazon in 1967, the region has been stripped of forests, covered with pools of black sludge and its Cofan indigenous nation brought to the brink of extinction.*

Dr. Robert Goodland, a former World Bank employee and author of many of their social and environmental guidelines, disagrees. His damning report concludes that the OCP study did not adhere to World Bank standards and was negligent in four important areas: Environmental Assessment, Natural Habitats, Involuntary Resettlement and Indigenous Peoples. According to Goodland, the OCP study did not adequately assess alternate routes; failed to assess the impact of increased oil development in the Amazon; and failed to minimize impact on environmentally sensitive areas including the Choco Forest (a World Bank protected zone). He concluded that the OCP consortium's compensation process, resettlement plans and its assessment of the project's impact on vulnerable ethnic groups were inadequate.

Indigenous communities, such as Sarayacu, have not

signed any agreements with OCP and have even detained sur-veyors and their armed guards to make the point that oil com-panies are not welcome. They know the next oil boom could spell the extinction of their way of life.

Already, forests and farms have been devastated, as the un-derground pipe requires a path the size of a two-lane road, as well as wide roads to allow heavy trucks in and out. And in April [2003], Quito residents got a rude awakening when the old pipeline burst, spilling 10,000 barrels of oil into one of the city's main water reservoirs. The spill will cost more than $1 million to clean up. Oil workers at the scene believe it was heavy equip-ment that damaged the old pipeline. The OCP consortium de-nies responsibility.

Pipeline Politics

Critics argue the pipeline project has also weakened Ecuador's democratic process and exacerbated corruption, alleging that public consultation was non-existent before the government signed the OCP deal in 2000 and ineffective afterwards. Alberto Acosta is an economist with Ecuador's Latin American Institute of Social Investigation. He has spent years following the politi-cal economy of oil in his country. He puts it this way, "Who-ever gains control over petroleum production gains the power of the state. Those who protest are threatened or attacked and damage to the environment increases dramatically alongside these political tensions."

> *This pipeline puts the reserve, the birds and our water source at risk.*

As Ecuador's first city of oil, Lago Agrio is home to the Ama-zonas Terminal, where oil will be collected, processed and heated for its journey to the coast. The platform lies in the path of city expansion and was hotly opposed by city residents. Maximo Abad, the city's mayor, explains "we unanimously op-posed the location of the platform because it was too close to human settlement."

But three months after the issue was closed in city council five councillors abruptly reversed their votes, and called for

Abad's resignation. Abad alleges that OCP officials "persuaded the councillors to change their minds in private meetings."

Exploiting Ecuadorian Communities

When I spoke to Alan Boras, spokesperson for EnCana, last spring [2003], he denied that the company is responsible for the growing political conflict in Ecuador. When asked for EnCana's response to the violence its operations were provoking, Boras answered: "social issues are the problem of the Ecuadorian government."

Ray Kohut of OCP assures me that Ecuador's environmental and human rights are in good hands. He is responsible for all compensation and is confident that the OCP consortium is the best deal for Ecuador. He is so convinced that the OCP is ahead of the pack on human rights that he dares me to guess how much of the original $1.1 billion budget is earmarked for communities. "Twenty, percent?" I naively reply. He is shocked: "No, $7 million!" That's a whopping 0.006% or a single day's oil revenue in the 20-year life of the pipe.

> *Already, forests and farms have been devastated, as the underground pipe requires a path the size of a two-lane road, as well as wide roads to allow heavy trucks in and out.*

Kohut denies the stories I've heard from locals. "Everything we do, we do publicly, word by word, put it in the newspaper," he says. "We give all information so that everybody knows what we're involved with, who's running with the ball."

This transparency was not evident to Canadian videographer Nadja Drost of Toronto Environmental Alliance when she tried to film a meeting between Kohut and the disgruntled villagers of El Reventador. The community is frantic because the pipeline crosses through their village. Last November [2002], the nearby volcano began spewing ash and causing mudslides. Scalding mud and rock scorched the pipeline and shifted it off its path. Locals want the OCP to move the pipe outside of town.

Kohut arrived in El Reventador in January 2003—along with two pick-up trucks full of police and soldiers. Soldiers blocked the entrance to the stadium where he met village representatives. They denied many residents entry, and would not allow Drost to film the event.

"Those who did gain entry were not able to speak," says Drost. "Mr. Kohut denied the request to move the pipe, signed a non-binding agreement for 'compensation,' patted a few farmers on the back and sped back to the safety of Quito, leaving many anxious for their future safety."

For OCP's opponents, fighting the development has become a war of attrition. Mayor Abad continues to lobby OCP to honour its compensation commitments and operate as safely as possible. Edwin, the nature guide, knows he cannot stop the pipeline now, but says he is working to ensure that every environmental i is dotted and t is crossed. He is part of a grassroots NGO [non-governmental organization] that has raised money to buy a part of the pipeline route in an effort to stall construction. His group keeps close tabs on the OCP and has had the consortium's environmental license revoked twice for illegal practices in Mindo.

Meanwhile, EnCana is listed in the portfolios of three Canadian "ethical funds" and assures its investors of solid growth in the coming year.

4

Oil Production Can Help to Protect Rain Forests

Center for International Forestry Research

The Center for International Forestry Research is an international research institution committed to conserving forests and improving the livelihoods of people in the tropics.

According to a new report by the Center for International Forestry Research (CIFOR), oil drilling and mining in tropical environments have helped to preserve rain forests. In Gabon, Africa, for example, the jobs and wealth generated by the oil industry have encouraged thousands of people to leave forested regions and move to cities. As a result, there has been a decrease in logging, farming, hunting, and other human activities that harm the rain forests of the country. The governments of developing countries can use their oil wealth to strengthen the urban economy and help people find jobs in cities instead of being forced to clear rain forests to grow crops or harvest their natural resources. However, companies should not view the CIFOR report as a license to use mining practices that cause excessive damage to the environment.

A new report released today [in June 2003] by one of the world's leading international forest research centers comes to the startling conclusion that producing oil and minerals actually helps some countries protect most of their forests and the exotic animal and plant species that live there. The report

Center for International Forestry Research "Cheap Oil on World Market Could Step Up Destruction of Rainforests in Tropics, Warns New Report," www.cifor.cgiar.org, June 23, 2003. Copyright © 2003 by the Center for International Forestry Research. Reproduced by permission.

was produced by the Indonesian-based Center for International Forestry Research (CIFOR). CIFOR does not receive funding from oil or mining companies.

Since practically one half of all tropical forests are in countries that rely heavily on petroleum and mineral exports for their incomes such as Venezuela, Gabon, Ecuador, Indonesia, and Papua New Guinea, this conclusion has huge implications. Over 12 million hectares of natural forest, corresponding to the size of Greece, are lost in the tropics every year.

"The prospect of Iraqi oil flooding the world market over the next few years and pushing down gasoline prices is music to the ears of consumers. But our research has found that it could be devastating for tropical forests," said Sven Wunder, author of the report, who is an economist at CIFOR.

The report, titled "Oil Wealth and the Fate of the Forest: A Comparison of Eight Tropical Countries," argues that high incomes from oil and minerals can relieve pressure on forests in several ways. High revenues from oil and mineral exports strengthen exporters' national currencies. The resulting changes in exchange rates makes it less attractive to invest in activities associated with forest-destruction such as farming in forested areas and logging. Oil-rich governments increase spending on urban development. That stimulates the urban economy and attracts people out of the jungle and into the cities, allowing forests to come back—or at least deforestation to go down, according to the report.

> *If people can earn more money from oil and mineral activities—or the government bureaucracies and construction booms they finance—those people are less likely to cut down forests to farm.*

"When developing countries get higher prices for their oil and mineral exports, it usually makes agriculture and logging less profitable," said Wunder. "If people can earn more money from oil and mineral activities—or the government bureaucracies and construction booms they finance—those people are less likely to cut down forests to farm."

When oil and mineral revenues fall and economic crisis follows, everything works in reverse, potentially causing widespread deforestation, says the report. Currencies weaken, making logging and the expansion of farming into forest areas more profitable. Unemployed urban workers move back to the countryside where they can hunt for bushmeat [from wild animals] and clear forests to grow crops.

> *The indirect, forest-protecting . . . effects oil wealth brings greatly outweigh the direct negative impacts associated with oil production and mining.*

Environmentalists have campaigned for years against the damage inflicted on forests by oil and mineral companies slashing through virgin jungle to build drilling platforms, worker camps, helipads, and access roads. According to the new report, however, such negative direct impacts resulting from mining and petroleum are only part of the story. "The indirect, forest-protecting macro-economic effects oil wealth brings greatly outweigh the direct negative impacts associated with oil production and mining. The crucial factor is how governments spend their oil wealth," Wunder said.

Other Types of Cash Infusions Also Protect Rain Forests

The implications of this analysis go far beyond minerals and petroleum. "The key lesson from this research is not that oil and mining are good for forests, but rather that changes in commodity prices, exchange rates, and wage rates frequently have a much greater impact on the environment than most people realize," said Wunder. "Even though these effects are indirect and invisible to the eye, they can actually be quite large."

Wunder points out that the positive impact on forests does not have to come only from an increase in oil or mineral wealth. Indeed, many types of capital inflows can have the same beneficial effects on forests as oil and mineral revenues. As Kristalina Georgieva, the Director of the World Bank's Environment Division, and author of the foreword to the report notes, "other international capital transfers, like bilateral credits, aid or debt relief, can have similar impacts" as oil and mineral revenues and can also help to alleviate pressures on forests.

"People have been arguing for some time about whether relieving the large level of foreign debt held by many developing countries would help them save their forests," said Wunder. CIFOR's study suggests in most cases it would, especially in the poorest countries of Africa. "This is also true of foreign direct investment or the money sent home by immigrants living in the United States or Europe," continued Wunder.

The results of CIFOR's study also lend weight to critics of economic austerity programs involving large currency devaluations. According to CIFOR's Director General, David Kaimowitz, "If developing countries are forced to devalue their national currencies as part of some International Monetary Fund program, this will make it much more profitable to cut down the forest. That may be good for the economy, but it spells trouble for forests."

Cases in Point: Gabon and Venezuela

Few countries illustrate the impact of oil wealth on rainforests better than the sparsely populated Central African nation of Gabon. Up until the 1970s, most Gabonese lived, farmed, and hunted in villages in the forest. After oil revenues shot up during the first oil crisis in the mid-1970s, however, people moved to the cities, giving up their thatched huts for suburban houses —and in the case of the elite, French champagne and high rise buildings of Libreville, the country's capital.

Most people living in Gabon, which came to be known as the "African Emirates," stopped farming and ate imported food instead. This has not necessarily been a wise development strategy, especially since oil resources are slowly drying up, which will make it necessary to develop alternative income sources.

But for forests, it has been excellent news, according to Wunder. In many rural areas of the interior, oil wealth has caused a dramatic rural exodus, and forests have grown back in abandoned fields. One village chief named Mbouila Thaopile described the process like this, "Nobody lives here anymore. The young are leaving and the elephants and gorillas run freely through our gardens, destroying what little we grow to eat."

As a result, "forest cover in Gabon has basically remained unchanged since 1970, probably with marginal net reforestation," according to the report, whereas the average tropical country loses its forest at a speed of about 1% per year.

In other cases the story is slightly different. In Venezuela, for example, when oil first became important back in the 1920s, the country initially went through a process similar to Gabon. People moved massively to the cities, abandoning the rural areas. Forest area markedly increased up to 1950. But, after World War II, unlike Gabon, the government used large amounts of its oil money to build roads into the jungle and promote cattle ranching, at the expense of forests. So, deforestation started to pick up, even though it remained much lower than in other forested countries. The difference for forests was how the governments used their oil wealth.

Given Wunder's controversial conclusion that oil and mineral exports can be good for forests, some critics might think that this report is out to promote the big oil companies. However, Wunder emphasizes that the positive indirect benefits for forests from oil and mining do not justify mining companies unnecessarily damaging the environment.

"Environmentalists should not misinterpret this report. The research in no way excuses companies using destructive mining practices that excessively damage the environment. But the report does say that unless governments adopt extremely land-extensive and forest-damaging policies, oil and mining will benefit forests through a range of powerful macroeconomic effects," Wunder said.

5

The Hunt for Bush Meat Threatens Wildlife in African Rain Forests

Bushmeat Crisis Task Force

The Bushmeat Crisis Task Force (BCTF) is a consortium of conservation organizations and scientists dedicated to the preservation of wildlife populations threatened by commercial hunting.

The Central African rain forest is the second largest in the world after the Amazon. This vast expanse of rain forest is threatened by exploding population growth in Central and West Africa. The inhabitants of these areas rely on bush meat, or the meat of wild animals, to meet their daily protein demands. Poor, rural families who live in the African tropics have few ways to earn money. They are thus greatly motivated by the high prices paid for bush meat to kill any animal they find in the jungle. Hunters ignore poorly enforced regulations out of desperation to survive. As a result, hunted animals—including gorillas, elephants, and bush pigs—are facing extinction. In some areas, all of the large animals have already disappeared because they were overhunted. This loss of wildlife damages the delicate ecosystem of the rain forest. Any effective policy to conserve the animals of the rain forest will have to take into account the needs of the poor families that are most dependent upon bush meat for survival.

In Africa, the forest and shrub land is often referred to as 'the bush', thus wildlife and the meat derived from that wildlife is locally called 'bushmeat' (in French—*viande de brousse*). This term applies to all wildlife species including: elephant, gorilla, chimpanzee and other primates, forest antelope (duikers), porcupine, bush pig, cane rat, pangolin, monitor lizard, guinea fowl, etc.

" Hunting for both local consumption and large commercial markets has become the most immediate threat to the future of wildlife in the Congo Basin. "

Over 24 million people live within the forested regions of Central Africa, 40–60% live in cities and towns, and most rely on the meat of wildlife as a primary source of animal protein. Forest antelope (duikers), pigs, and primates are most often eaten, and as much as 1 million metric tons of wildlife is killed for food in Central Africa each year. In West African nations human population densities are high (25–78 persons per square kilometer) compared to countries in the Congo Basin (5–20 persons per square kilometer). West African wildlife populations have been so depleted by years of unsustainable hunting for meat, that bushmeat is no longer the most important source of protein in families' diets. When bushmeat is eaten, ungulates and primates have been replaced by rodents as the most commonly eaten wild animals.

Though deforestation and habitat loss are often cited as the primary causes of local wildlife extinction, hunting for both local consumption and large commercial markets has become the most immediate threat to the future of wildlife in the Congo Basin in the next 5–15 years. It has already resulted in widespread local extinctions throughout the Upper Guinea Forest Ecosystem of West Africa.

The Empty Forest Syndrome

Hunting of wildlife to meet people's demand for protein may still be sustainable in the few remaining areas where population densities are less than two people per square kilometer, trade routes are poorly established, and human population growth rates are low. The scale of the commercial bushmeat trade now occurring in West and Central Africa is driven by markets with high human densities and growth rates. This commercial market threatens the survival of many species, including several unique to the dense forested regions of Africa. While deforestation is an obvious menace to wildlife dependent on these habitats, hunting constitutes a comparable threat to the ecosystem itself. Even where tree cover is relatively intact, we find forests with no large animals—this is known as Empty Forest Syndrome.

Absence of animals because they were over-hunted for bushmeat will result in the loss of predators such as leopard, golden cats, large snakes and birds of prey that depend on them for food. Loss of wildlife also means a loss of seed dispersing animals that play a key role in determining tree composition and distribution, causing, over the long term, loss of many plant species, altering both the structure and function of the forest and potentially causing irreversible ecological effects (e.g., carbon sequestration) with global consequences.

> *Absence of animals because they were over-hunted for bushmeat will result in the loss of predators such as leopard, golden cats, large snakes and birds of prey that depend on them for food.*

While poor families can derive short-term economic benefits from the commercial bushmeat trade, the unsustainable trade in wildlife will jeopardize long-term economic opportunities and cultural traditions for future generations. In addition, increasing levels of contact with wildlife populations may place people in increased jeopardy of contracting and transmitting animal-derived diseases such as Ebola or HIV, and risks transmitting human diseases that may be lethal to apes and other species.

Growing Demand for Meat and Limited Productivity of Wildlife

Urban populations in Central and West Africa are growing at 2–4% per year and only 1–2% of that is from rural to urban migration. Urban families typically consume more resources than their relatively poor rural relatives, and it is likely that demand for bushmeat will increase by 2–4% per year—a rate that far exceeds the replacement potential of already over-hunted wildlife populations.

Wildlife populations, though highly diverse in these forests, are not as productive when compared with savanna-based wildlife populations. In general, there is an order of magnitude difference between the biomass available for hunting within the same amount of space when we compare forests (2,500 kg per square kilometer) and savannahs (25,000 kilograms per square kilometer). Thus, animal husbandry programs such as the game ranching efforts (commercial management of wildlife for meat and skins) found in East and Southern Africa are not necessarily a viable alternative in West and Central Africa.

In the region, domestic animals such as cattle, goats, pigs, chickens and ducks are raised by rural and urban households, but they are primarily viewed as savings and insurance rather than as sources of protein. This traditional value of livestock remains important to households in the region today because inflation is high and access to banks and formal credit is limited or absent. Furthermore, tsetse flies and trypanosomiasis severely limit cattle raising in the forested and scrubby savanna landscapes typical of the region. As a result, the meat of domestic livestock tends only to appear in rural or urban markets that are located relatively close to savannas and ethnic groups with a tradition of pastoralism.

Hunting Is Profitable in the Short Term

In the Congo Basin, collapsing roads systems and declining global prices for traditional cash crops such as coffee and cocoa have left rural families with fewer and fewer ways to make money sufficient to meet basic needs for food, shelter, clothing, schooling and health, at a time when government spending on social services is decreasing per capita. Bushmeat with its relatively high value to transportation cost ratio offers poor rural families a lucrative, if short-term, source of money. Moreover, hunting and trading bushmeat can be scheduled so as not to compete with other household activities such as farming or fishing, so the opportunity costs of participating in the bushmeat trade are often not significant. When wildlife are abundant hunters can make between $400 and $1100 per year from bushmeat alone, which exceeds the average income for households across the region, and is comparable or greater than the salaries of guards paid to prevent hunting. In West Africa, although wildlife is less abundant, the price of meat and the low opportunity costs to hunting, ensure that the bushmeat trade remains profitable. Consequently there remain strong economic incentives for families in West and Central Africa to participate in the commercial trade in bushmeat.

> *Gorillas may be targeted explicitly by hunters because gorilla hands are considered a delicacy by some consumers.*

If only one species of animal existed in the forest, hunters would continue to hunt that species until it became so scarce that profits from hunting would decline below that which the hunter could make doing something else, such as farming or fishing. Unfortunately for rare and endangered species, the forests of West and Central Africa are home to numerous wildlife species that are hunted for food. In this case, when people go hunting they are not targeting single species, but are roaming the forest in search of any animal worth (in economic terms) killing. A bushmeat hunter with a shotgun is inclined to shoot the largest animal he can be assured of killing because this will generate the most profit per cartridge. So although an animal may become scarce, even to the point of local extinction, a hunter will shoot it if he encounters it, and it is large enough to warrant using up an expensive shotgun cartridge. Given this fact, rare and endangered species are likely to be driven to extinction by hunters when other more abundant animals continue to make hunting profitable.

Hunting Animals to Extinction

In addition to the extinction threat from hunting with guns, the majority of bushmeat hunting taking place in the Congo Basin using wire snares with wastage rates (*i.e.* animals never make it to market due to rotting on the snare) ranging from 25%–94%. Such hunting methods are inhumane, unselective and highly unsustainable. They cause enormous losses across the range of mammalian species. Many animals are caught in snares and manage to escape but often with life-threatening injuries.

Moreover, even when over hunting and bushmeat scarcity causes prices to rise and substitutes to be more competitive, hunting will continue in areas where bushmeat capture and transport costs remain comparable to the costs of livestock rearing.

Duikers (small forest antelope), pigs, primates and rodents are the most commonly hunted groups of animals in the forest, with duikers both numerically and in terms of biomass being the most important bushmeat species group. Apes are most often hunted opportunistically and tend to constitute the 'bycatch' of hunters seeking the more abundant and, in absolute terms, more lucrative duikers. This is not surprising as gorillas are considered to be the most dangerous species to hunt. On occasion, gorillas may be targeted explicitly by hunters because gorilla hands are considered a delicacy by some consumers. Apes' absolute scarcity and low reproductive rates means that, though they rarely constitute more than 1% of the carcasses brought into markets, even present levels of hunting may threaten the long term survival of all ape populations within all range states in the Congo Basin. In long established markets in the Congo Basin and throughout West Africa, rodents appear to gain in importance presumably because duikers and primates have been depleted in nearby forests.

Commercial Logging Increases
Hunter and Market Access

In the Congo Basin region of Central Africa, valuable trees species are scattered in low density throughout the forest. To find and harvest these trees, loggers construct numerous survey trails and roads, heavily fragmenting the forest, and opening it up to hunters. The large numbers of workers employed by the logging company eat more meat than poorer unemployed families, they have the money to purchase weapons, they have ready access to the forest to hunt, and to logging trucks to transport meat. Consequently, logging companies not only directly increase demand for meat by hiring a large workforce; they also greatly facilitate workers' entry into the commercial trade to supply bushmeat to urban markets. This same scenario played itself out in West Africa in the 1950s and 1960s, and contributed to the regional decline in wildlife populations evident in West African forests today.

A major factor enabling the uncontrolled advance of the commercial bushmeat trade is the lack of capacity to enforce existing national and international legislation. Much of the hunting taking place throughout the region is illegal. There are limited personnel and infrastructure to effectively address the needs for control of hunting and the bushmeat trade throughout the West and Central African region. Confounding this fact is the reality that policies and laws that are intended to regulate the hunting of wildlife are seldom perceived by local communities as legitimate, desirable, or enforceable and are therefore widely ignored.

Poverty and Policy

Commercial bushmeat hunting is one of the few currently available income generating options for many rural families. Poverty, coupled with economic and civil instability within the region, makes efforts to curb such hunting politically difficult. Moreover, convincing hunters to change their behavior because forest wildlife are globally scarce is easier said than done, as hunters view the same wildlife as being locally abundant, and free for the taking. The bushmeat trade involves complex networks of rural and urban producers—any effective policy developments will require an understanding of the role each group of participants play within the trade.

The role of policy makers and policy making at the local, national and international level is to reconcile the trade-off between resource over-exploitation for short-term economic gain and the irreplaceable loss of biodiversity. So what makes a good policy? In the best circumstances natural resource management policy making is based on consensus and compromise, because, given the different needs and priorities of all stakeholders, only when the majority of the people that a policy affects are equally "happy" can a policy be said to be good. From the opposite perspective, a policy is bad because it fails to address the concerns, needs and priorities of stakeholders who have the ability to prevent or subvert effective implementation of the policy.

Given present and projected demand for bushmeat, policies to conserve wildlife are likely to impose resource use restrictions that will directly impact the household economies of families involved in the commercial bushmeat trade—be they producers, traders, or consumers. Conservation by its very nature imposes short-term costs for long-term benefits, and often results in short term sacrifices to meet long-term local, national or international needs. Poor families are often most dependent on natural resources such as bushmeat, and will suffer most from the implementation of restrictions on their use. Consequently, they should be considered as one of the most important stakeholders in bushmeat management policy making, and should be compensated for any economic losses associated with conserving wildlife.

Solutions to the Bushmeat Crisis

Awareness and support for control of the bushmeat trade was virtually non-existent until the late 1990's. Careful science and the efforts of a few key individuals began to change that, and NGOs [nongovernmental organizations], governments, and the private sector are now rising to the challenge with increased funding and innovative solutions.

In the U.S., zoological institutions, animal protection and international conservation organizations joined together to collaborate on this issue through the Bushmeat Crisis Task Force (BCTF), founded in 1999. BCTF members work individually to support actions in the field that directly address human and wildlife impacts of the bushmeat crisis, and work together through the BCTF project to share and manage information in support of U.S. and international efforts to engage with key decision makers (KDMs) in government and industry, facilitate relevant education and training efforts, and raise public awareness. BCTF frequently provides information to U.S. government agencies on appropriate policies related to bushmeat, helps member organizations present the issue to the public and their memberships, and maintains an information management system, physical library and expert network in support of information requests from policy makers, journalists, students and researchers from around the world. For more information, visit www.bushmeat.org.

BCTF has the capacity to focus on selected solutions needed to curb the bushmeat crisis. The major solutions areas, categorized below, need to be implemented at some level simultaneously and for the long-term to effectively address the bushmeat crisis and assure that wildlife, local communities and the ecosystems they depend upon will continue to exist for future generations.

Information Management: Accurate and timely information is critical to planning and implementing responses to the crisis. Information technology increases opportunities for communications, collaboration, and consensus building. Fact sheets, newsletters, synthesis papers, books, maps, databases, discussion lists, and websites have been instrumental in bringing the bushmeat crisis to the attention of KDMs and the public in developed and developing countries throughout the world.

Education and Training: Public education and targeted training raises support for solutions as well as the capacity to implement them. In recent years, bushmeat training has been added to the curriculum of wildlife management training programs in Africa, and national parks and NGOs are already benefiting from these developments. U.S. zoos are including bushmeat messages in public programs, exhibit signage and docent presentations, and African primate sanctuaries have greatly expanded their capacity for education on the bushmeat issue.

> *Logging companies not only directly increase demand for meat by hiring a large workforce; they also greatly facilitate workers' entry into the commercial trade to supply bushmeat to urban markets.*

Public Awareness: Public awareness campaigns in the wealthy countries of the world are essential to educate international consumers about the bushmeat crisis, to gain support for projects and policies and to educate about forest products that are harvested irresponsibly, from wood and paper to bushmeat and ivory. Other campaigns are needed for the wholly different audience of bushmeat traders and consumers, who are unaware of relevant laws and bushmeat alternatives. The challenge of such campaigns is to assure the distinction between sustainable, legal, subsistence-level hunting that enables rural communities to meet basic protein needs and unsustainable, illegal, commercial level hunting that jeopardizes such opportunities for future generations. Without appropriate law enforcement and other solutions, populations that depend on subsistence hunting may lose access to their resources due to overhunting.

Engaging with Key Decision Makers: Key decision makers (KDMs) are those senior level individuals with decision-making authority in government, non-profit organizations, communities, and the private sector who have an essential role in enabling long-term wildlife conservation. Their policies on resource use provide the frameworks around which day to day decisions are made concerning the use of wildlife. It is essential that KDMs are aware of the various issues related to the bushmeat crisis and are able to identify how they can most effectively play a role in addressing it. The international *Congo Basin Forest Partnership* is a high-profile example of what can result from a partnership forged by leaders in governments, NGOs, business and academia.

Law Enforcement: Much of the bushmeat trade is unsustainable because existing laws are not adequately enforced. In many African countries, protected area boundaries are porous to hunters, protected species are not monitored in the markets or the forests, and hunting of legal species in legal areas is done with illegal weapons (especially wire snares) and/or out of season. With support from local and international civil society, some governments are starting to step up enforcement in city markets, improve protected area management and monitoring, and confiscate illegal species and weapons. Many countries still need to create or modify laws and law enforcement structures to address this issue.

Economic and Protein Alternatives: Wildlife law enforcement is more effective and accepted when there are alternative foods for bushmeat consumers and alternative income opportunities for hunters and traders. These should be culturally and environmentally appropriate and economically competitive with bushmeat. Economic and agricultural development strategies could focus on the needs of people most dependent on wildlife, who are frequently the most marginalized and needy by any measure. From broad fair trade initiatives for coffee and cocoa to small-scale business and industry (including ecotourism) to specific projects to raise domestic livestock and even cane rats, a range of recent efforts have shown promise. These small- and mid-size steps will ideally be complemented by national-level debt relief, foreign investment and opening up of high GDP [gross domestic product] markets to low GDP country goods.

Networking and Capacity Building: Developing wildlife and land management capacity at local, national, and regional levels is highly important. All stakeholders should focus efforts to assure that the necessary governmental and financial support for protected area management exists, law enforcement capabilities are in place, and broad-based initiatives toward working with and educating the public are implemented. These actions can be encouraged through building partnerships with the private sector, government, conservation agencies and local communities.

Private Sector Partnerships: Working to improve the environmental sustainability of businesses operating in wildlife-rich areas has many benefits, whether they are oil companies or oil palm growers. In the Congo Basin, developing wildlife management activities with logging companies may provide the most effective intervention in the near-term because of their key role in the commercial bushmeat trade and the large areas of forest for which they have management responsibilities. Pilot collaborations between NGOs and logging companies have demonstrated the potential for success, as well as the necessary conditions and activities: effective systems for monitoring wildlife; incentives for company employees, other local residents, and government to negotiate and implement the regulation of wildlife use; and disincentives for these same stakeholders to flout agreed upon regulations. Other activities will facilitate this process, including: providing alternative sources of protein for employees; linking bonuses to compliance with wildlife regulations; preferentially employing local residents; restricting human immigration into concessions; negotiating forest areas to be left intact; prohibiting use of logging vehicles to transport bushmeat; and removing bridges and roads in already logged areas.

Protected Areas, Zoning and Land Management: Long-term support for protected areas, including provision of well-equipped and trained anti-poaching units, is a clear priority for mitigating the commercial bushmeat trade. The number and size of protected areas should be increased where appropriate, and management and financing for these should be enhanced. This is particularly true for West Africa where much of the original forest cover has been removed and protected areas provide some of the only land available for many wildlife populations.

Current systems of logging and mining concession allocation should be reviewed in terms of long-term benefits and sustainability of activities. Indigenous people should receive clear land and resource rights as prescribed by national and international laws. Illegal hunting, mining and logging camps should not be acknowledged and elevated as towns and ultimately cities, increasing the human population in areas with high wildlife value and low social and health service infrastructure.

6

Cattle Ranching Is Destroying Brazil's Rain Forest

David Kaimowitz et al.

David Kaimowitz is the director general of the Center for International Forestry Research (CIFOR), an international research institution committed to conserving forests and improving the livelihoods of people in the tropics. Benoit Mertens, formerly of CIFOR, is currently the Cameroon Project Coordinator for Global Forest Watch, an organization formed to manage and conserve forests. Sven Wunder is the senior economist at CIFOR and the author of Oil Wealth and the Fate of the Forest. *Pablo Pacheco is a sociologist, agricultural economist, and author who has worked for CIFOR and other organizations dedicated to preserving rain forests.*

The growing worldwide demand for Brazilian beef is creating unprecedented damage to the Amazon rain forest. Brazilians are now cutting down more than 6.1 million acres of rain forest a year and converting it to grazing land for cows. This land, because of its poor soil, is able to support cattle grazing for only a few years. Then more deforestation must take place to feed the cows. The Brazilian government is taking steps to prevent deforestation, such as better land use planning and enforcement of laws against deforestation. However, stronger measures are needed to prevent the destruction of the rain forest.

David Kaimowitz, Benoit Mertens, Sven Wunder, and Pablo Pacheco, "Hamburger Connection Fuels Amazon Destruction: Cattle Ranching and Deforestation in Brazil's Amazon," www.cifor.cgair.org, April 2004. Copyright © 2004 by the Center for International Forestry Research. Reproduced by permission.

This report explains the link between . . . [the] frightening increase in deforestation [in the Brazilian Amazon] and the growth in international demand for Brazilian beef. It also calls on the international community to provide urgent assistance. Brazil's beef exports have grown markedly due to the devaluation of the Brazilian currency and factors related to animal diseases such as foot and mouth disease, mad cow disease (Bovine Spongiform Encephalopathy), and the avian flu.

While many analysts have previously discussed the link between cattle ranching and deforestation in the Amazon, until now the main concern has been production for sale within Brazil. Until this report, very little attention has been given to the role played by the international demand for Brazilian beef in rapidly escalating Brazil's loss of Amazonian rainforest.

> *In just ten years the country lost an area of forest twice the size of Portugal or the size of Uruguay.*

The accumulated area of deforestation in the Brazilian Amazon rose from 41.5 million hectares [102 million acres] in 1990 to 58.7 million hectares [145 million acres] in 2000. In just ten years the country lost an area of forest twice the size of Portugal or the size of Uruguay. In the two years after the alarmingly high level of deforestation in 1994–95, analysts were optimistic rates were starting to fall. However, they began rising again in 1997–98 and then skyrocketed in 2002.

Cattle and Deforestation

The overwhelming majority of the forest area lost in the Brazilian Amazon eventually becomes pasture. According to the most recent census figures available, the area of land devoted to crops in 1995–96 amounted to 5,608,000 hectares [13.9 million acres] while the figure for pasture was 33,579,000 [82.9 million acres].

In other words, for every one hectare of cropland there were almost six hectares of pasture. Nothing suggests that pattern has changed since 1996. . . .

Although the last few years have witnessed a great deal of

justifiable concern about the expansion of soybean cultivation into the Amazon, that still explains only a small percentage of total deforestation. The total area of soybeans in the Legal Amazon in 2002 was only 4.9 million hectares [12 million acres], while the area in pasture was almost certainly more than ten times that amount. Moreover, much of the soybean area is in the savanna region of Mato Grosso and in places that have been deforested for many years. Only a relatively small percentage represents new forest clearing.

Logging rarely leads directly to deforestation in the Amazon. Most loggers only remove a small number of trees per hectare. That often damages the forest but it does not destroy it. Logging does contribute indirectly to deforestation by making it easier for forests to catch fire and for farmers to move into forested areas. However, logging is much less damaging than the growth of cattle ranching.

Massive Growth in Amazon's Cattle Numbers

Cattle expansion in the Amazon in the last twelve years has been phenomenal. During this period, the number of cattle more than doubled, from 26 million in 1990 to 57 million in 2002. In the process it has gone from representing 17.8% of Brazil's total cattle herd to almost one third. In fact, 80% of all of the growth in Brazil's livestock population in this period was in the Amazon. The overwhelming majority of the new cattle are concentrated in Brazil's Amazon states of Mato Grosso, Pará, and Rondônia, which were also the states with the greatest deforestation in 2002.

Beef Exports: The Hamburger Connection

Back in the early 1980s, well-known environmentalist, Norman Myers, coined the phrase "the hamburger connection". The phrase described how the rapid growth of beef exports from Central America to fast food chains in the United States was driving deforestation. At the time, however, the term did not apply to Brazil, as the country exported little beef and most of the beef produced in the Amazon was consumed within the region itself.

The Amazon region did not even produce enough beef to feed its own population until 1991. After that the region began to produce a growing surplus of beef for the national market, but Brazilian beef exports to other countries continued to play a minor role. At the time, [according to scholar M.D. Faminow] Brazil experienced a strong "domestic hamburger connection", affecting initially the Atlantic forest and later the Amazon. Brazilian beef consumption quadrupled between 1972 and 1997. Much of this was led by growing urban incomes, causing per capita meat consumption to more than double over the same time span.

> *Some experts claim that Brazil now ranks as the world's largest beef exporter.*

As recently as 1995, Brazil exported less than $500 million dollars of beef. By 2003, only eight years later, Brazil was exporting three times as much, $1.5 billion dollars. Between 1997 and 2003, the volume of exports increased more than fivefold, from 232,000 to nearly 1.2 million metric tons in carcass weight equivalence.

Meanwhile, domestic beef consumption, which for decades has been responsible for the sector's expansion, developed slowly. For the first time ever, the growth in Brazilian livestock production—80% of which was in the Amazon—was largely export driven. Although there is no consolidated data available on the ranking of exports for 2003, some experts claim that Brazil now ranks as the world's largest beef exporter.

What Drives Brazilian Beef Exports?

Currency Devaluations

One major factor that has been driving the rise in Brazilian beef exports—and Amazon deforestation—has been the massive devaluation of the national currency, the real, from 1.2 reais [plural of real] per dollar in December 1998, to 3.6 reais per dollar in December 2002. As a result, the price of beef in Brazilian reais approximately doubled in that period, creating a huge incentive for ranchers to expand their pasture area. At the same time, the price of Brazilian beef in dollars has fallen, which has made Brazil's exports more competitive on international markets.

Several studies in the past had already predicted that large currency devaluations would lead to a major increase in agricultural and livestock driven deforestation. These studies use macro-economic models known as Computable General Equilibrium models to simulate how changes in exchange rates might affect land use—and hence deforestation. The most sophisticated and recent of these studies, by Andrea Cattaneo, predicted that under the most realistic set of assumptions a 40% real devaluation of the Brazilian currency would increase deforestation by 20% once markets adjusted.

Livestock Disease Trends

For many years the presence of foot and mouth (FMD) disease in most of Brazil had kept the country from exporting its beef products to many international markets. Prior to 1998, no Brazilian state had been certified as being free of the disease. That year the two southern states of Rio Grande do Sul and Santa Catarina were declared free of FMD. Since then the certified area has expanded greatly. As of 2003, 85% of the country's cattle herd was in areas that had been certified as not having FMD. Between 1994 and 2002 the proportion of cattle vaccinated against the disease rose from 64% to 86%.

> *Farmers find it easy to illegally occupy government land without being prosecuted, and to deforest areas much larger than the 20% of their farms currently permitted by law.*

Most of the country has now been certified as free of FMD. This has greatly helped Brazil to gain access to a number of new markets in Europe, Russia, and the Middle East. Between 1990 and 2001, the percentage of Europe's transformed meat imports that came from Brazil rose from 40% to 74%.

The improvement in the FMD situation has been particularly important for stimulating Amazon beef production. Once some federal states in the south were certified as being FMD-free in 1998, other states that still had FMD—including all of the Amazonian states—were restricted from sending any beef products to FMD-free areas, except for meat that had been deboned. That made it much more difficult for the Amazon's ranchers to sell beef to the country's large urban markets such as São Paolo or Rio de Janeiro, much less export it abroad.

Now, however, the situation has changed. Since 2003 the states of Mato Grosso, Rondônia, and Tocantins have been declared FMD-free, and can now sell their beef any where they want. These states account for over 60% of the region's cattle herd. By 2005, the Brazilian government expects the entire country to be declared free of the disease. These changes have increased beef prices in the Amazon, and hence the incentive to deforest.

Problems outside Brazil with Mad Cow disease (BSE) and the avian flu have also encouraged beef exports. Many countries banned beef imports from Canada and the United States after several BSE cases were discovered in 2003, and avian flu problems in Asia reduced poultry exports from those countries. This resulted in some consumers switching to beef from Brazil.

// *Unless urgent action is taken, the Brazilian Amazon will probably lose an additional area the size of Denmark [by 2006].* **//**

Other Changes in the Amazon
The previously mentioned changes in exchange rates and livestock diseases have given much greater force to Amazonian dynamics that were already underway. These include the rapid expansion of the region's road and electricity network and large investments in modern new slaughterhouses and meatpacking and dairy plants. Very low land prices in the Amazon also help to make ranching profitable. These prices remain very low in part because farmers find it easy to illegally occupy government land without being prosecuted, and to deforest areas much larger than the 20% of their farms currently permitted by law.

What Must Be Done?

On March 15th [2004], Brazil's President Luis Inácio (Lula) da Silva announced a major new "Action Plan to Prevent and Control Deforestation in the Legal Amazon". The Action Plan commits the government to spending 394 million reais (approximately $135 million dollars US) on activities designed to reduce deforestation. These include: land use planning, greater enforcement of laws concerning deforestation and the illegal occupation of government lands, deforestation monitoring, reviews of public infrastructure investments, support for indigenous territories and community forestry, support for sustainable agriculture, and greater control over credit for ranchers, among others.

> *Unfortunately, given the current recession in the Brazilian economy, it will be very difficult for the government to allocate the level of resources needed to save the Amazon.*

The government's approach goes in the right direction. However, any strategies to effectively tackle the deforestation problem will require a number of additional measures, as well as more funds, greater coordination between and within the key ministries and regular high level attention. The international and domestic market forces currently promoting livestock-driven deforestation in Brazil described in this report are much stronger than ever. Even with the most determined policy response, decisively curbing deforestation may be difficult. To limit the negative impact on Brazil's Amazonian rainforests will require a massive effort in response. Unless urgent action is taken, the Brazilian Amazon will probably lose an additional area the size of Denmark [by 2006]. . . .

Recommendations

CIFOR [Center for International Forestry Research] recommends the following four policy areas as vital to the sustainable future of Brazil's Amazon forests:

1. Stop the land grabbing. The government's focus on land tenure regulation in its new Action Plan is fully justified. Making progress in this area will require substantial political will, appropriate levels of funding, and more efficient institutional mechanisms for keeping ranchers from illegally occupying government lands.
2. Restrict road projects outside already developed regions. The plans for new infrastructure, in particular road construction and improvement projects, need to be revised or reversed if deforestation really is to receive a high pri-

ority. Extensive studies on deforestation underline not only the absolutely key role roads play, but also the difficulty in implementing measures to control land speculation and deforestation close to roads.

3. Formally register government owned lands as National Forests (FLONAS) to stop the further incursion of ranching into these areas. For this purpose the Brazilian government should prioritize forested areas facing the greatest danger of being converted to pasture.

4. Provide economic incentives to maintain land as forest. Brazil already has a small compensation program to promote more intensive and eco-friendly agriculture (PRO-AMBIENTE), but it should also experiment with direct payments for forest conservation.

Implementing the measures needed to effectively reduce deforestation will require more resources than the Brazilian government has so far been able to commit. Unfortunately, given the current [2004] recession in the Brazilian economy, it will be very difficult for the government to allocate the level of resources needed to save the Amazon. The international community must be prepared to provide additional support to the Brazilian government's efforts.

7

Loggers and Ranchers Are Murdering Rain Forest Activists

Andrew Buncombe

This viewpoint by Andrew Buncombe appeared in the Asia Africa Intelligence Wire, *a publication that offers news and analysis of Asian, African, and Middle Eastern events, markets, and politics.*

People working to preserve the South American rain forests stand opposed to an extremely hostile group of ranchers and loggers who engage in a variety of illegal acts ranging from slavery to murder. In 1988 cattle ranchers murdered forest worker Chico Mendez, who organized Brazil's rubber tappers to fight against the destruction of rubber-producing rain forests. In February 2005 loggers killed a seventy-four-year-old American nun, Sister Dorothy Stang, who worked to preserve the rain forests in Brazil. Hundreds of less-well-known locals have also been killed in the struggle to save the forests. Some human rights groups argue that the Brazilian government is not adequately protecting the people who speak out and work against the destruction of the rain forests.

The Dominican nun lived among those who wanted her dead.

When they finally came for her she read passages from the Bible to her killers. They listened for a moment, took a step back and fired at her from point-blank range. Her body was face-down in the mud, blood staining the back of her white blouse.

The town of Anapu, on the edge of the Amazon rainforest, is most notable for the dust that clogs its streets and for the number of shops selling chainsaws.

It is also the place that Sister Dorothy Stang called home for more than 30 years and where she organised her efforts to protect the rainforest and its people from disastrous and often illegal exploitation by logging firms and ranchers. Now Anapu will be known as the place where Dorothy is buried.

The 74-year-old activist was buried this week [February 2005] after being assassinated by two gunmen last Saturday at a remote encampment in the jungle about 50km from the town. Dorothy—the most prominent activist to be murdered in the Amazon since the killing of Chico Mendez in 1988—was shot six times in the head, throat and body.

Nilde Sousa, an official with a local women's group who worked with the nun, said, "She was on a list of people marked for death. And little by little they're ticking these names off the list." As with the death of Mendez, a rubber-tapper, the murder of Dorothy has triggered waves of outrage among the activist community who say she dedicated her life to helping the area's poor, landless peasants and confronting the businesses that saw the rainforest purely as a resource to be plundered and which have already destroyed 20 percent of its 4 million square kilometres. It has also highlighted the problem for the Brazilian Government of balancing a desire to protect the rainforest with pressure to open tracts of forest to support strong economic growth as demanded by the International Monetary Fund, which lent Brazil billions of dollars after a recession in 2002. Such a conflict of interests has hindered attempts by the authorities to fulfil the promise of left-leaning President Luiz Inacio Lula da Silva to find homes for 400,000 landless families.

The promise is badly off-target and showing no signs of rapid improvement.

Little Doubt About Who the Killers Are

The President immediately ordered a full-scale investigation of Dorothy's death and dispatched two members of his Cabinet to the region, an area that is notorious for violence, crime and slave labour. One of those who was sent, Nilmario Miranda, the Government's Secretary for Human Rights, said before setting off, "Solving this crime and apprehending those who ordered and committed it is a question of honour for us. This is intolerable." Dorothy was in the Boa Esperanca settlement when she was killed. She was travelling with two peasants to a meeting to discuss a settlement for the area, which has apparently been granted to peasants by the Federal Government but which is sought by loggers. The two men travelling with her escaped unhurt and may have been able to identify the killers to police, according to reports.

> **// She was on a list of people marked for death. And little by little they're ticking those names off the list. //**

While the suspects' names have not yet been disclosed, Dorothy's supporters say there is little doubt as to who they are. While the local people called her Dora or "the angel of the Trans-Amazonian", loggers and other opponents called her a "terrorist" and accused her of supplying guns to the peasants. The Pastoral Land Commission of the Roman Catholic Church, which she worked for, said in a statement, "The hatred of ranchers and loggers respects nothing. The reprehensible murder of our sister brings back to us memories of a past that we had thought was closed." Dorothy was originally from Dayton, Ohio, where she attended Julienne High School. It was while she was a student that she decided to become a nun and when she left school she joined the convent of the Sisters of Notre Dame de Namur in Cincinnati. The order, founded in France in the early 18th century by Marie Rose Julia Billiart, is a proponent of liberation theology and social justice. Its mission statement dedicates the order to "take our stand with poor people, especially women and children, in the abandoned places".

Her beliefs took her to Brazil in the 1960s and it was there, in the vast Para region that encompasses large tracts of the rainforest, that she found her calling, despite the obvious dangers she faced.

[In February 2005], Dorothy met minister Miranda and told him of the death threats that she and others had received and asked for the Government's help and protection.

Sister Elizabeth Bowyer, a senior nun at the Cincinnati convent, said that she believed Dorothy might have realised she was going to be killed at some point even though she told her friends and colleagues that her status as a nun would offer a level of protection. "She knew she was on the death list," she said. "She said she would be protected because of her age and because she was a nun—she was wrong. We don't know who hired the gunmen but we know the loggers and ranchers were very upset by what she was doing. She was working with the human-rights people to protect the small farmers who have been given the right to the land." The stakes could not have been higher. Greenpeace [an environmental activist group] estimates that 90 percent of the timber in Para is illegally logged. The danger of speaking out against such exploitation could barely have been greater. Campaigners say Para has the country's highest rate of deaths related to land battles.

Greenpeace said that more than 40 percent of the murders between 1985 and 2001 were related to such disputes.

The Brazilian human-rights group Justice Global said 73 rural workers were murdered in 2003—33 of them in Para. Last year [2004] 53 were killed, 19 of them in Para. The group's director, Sandra Carvalho, says, "The Government is simply not giving adequate protection.

"We think its actions in the region are extremely weak. The Government put together a program to deal with these problems but it is being carried out at such a slow pace.

"The Government has not managed to carry out the land reforms it spelled out before coming to power. What they have done is far below what we anticipated." She added, "There is constant conflict with very few convictions because there is a culture of impunity.

"Generally these conflicts involve landowners and landless rural workers . . . Dora was killed because she stood up to these people." And yet this fight appeared to energise the sprightly 74-year-old.

Incredible Energy, Incredible Battles

Samuel Clements, 24, a student film-maker from Britain who spent the summer of 2003 filming Dorothy's work, said she seemed to become a different, more animated person once she left dusty Anapu and went into the jungle to meet the small farmers and peasants. In addition to fighting to preserve the rainforest she was helping encourage small-scale, sustainable agriculture.

In a recent letter to Clements, she wrote, "Our forest is being overtaken by the others daily. . . . Together we can make a difference." Clements also believed Dorothy might have had a premonition of the fate that awaited her and yet she still looked for the best in people. "She said once, 'Humanity is like a fruit bowl, with all the different fruit—black, white and yellow—so different and yet all part of it.' She had incredible energy even though she was fighting incredible battles," he said.

> **She said she would be protected because of her age and because she was a nun—she was wrong.**

Lucio Flavio Pinto, an investigative journalist in the region who produces a weekly newspaper, *Jornal Pessoal*, has known Dorothy since the 1970s. He has also been campaigning against the same people she was taking on and has also been on the receiving end of threats. "There were many people who wanted to kill Sister Dorothy," he said, speaking from the city of Belem, the state capital.

It was to Belem that Dorothy's body was taken on Sunday for a post-mortem examination and where dozens of supporters gathered outside the mortuary singing hymns and holding placards calling for an end to the rampant crime. Claudio Guimaraes, director of the state's forensic-science institute, said it appeared that the gunmen were about 435cm away from Dorothy when they shot her.

In Ohio she was remembered at a series of services at which her dedication and courage were mentioned. Father Dennis Caylor, pastor at St Rafael church in the suburb of Springfield said, "Sister Dorothy in her ministering to the poor remained faithful. We honour those who die for their faith." And from those who worked with the nun, there were promises that the effort she had undertaken would continue despite her death.

Mariana Silva, president of Brazil's National Institute for Settlement Agrarian Reform said, "We won't step back even one millimetre from our projects in Para because of this. They want to intimidate us but they won't succeed."

8

Business Leaders and Environmentalists Are Working Together to Preserve Rain Forests

Christopher M. Wille

Christopher M. Wille is the head of the Sustainable Agriculture Program for the Rainforest Alliance, an organization that works to protect the environment by transforming land-use practices, business practices, and consumer behavior.

Environmentalists and corporations have often been at odds with one another. However, the traditional conflict between those wishing to protect the environment and those wishing to profit from it has been transformed in recent years. Independent citizen organizations, called nongovernmental organizations, or NGOs, have been working with agricultural and logging companies to change business practices that damage rain forests. This cooperation has resulted in better treatment of indigenous workers, less pesticide use, and the protection of rain forests. Companies also benefit by improving their corporate image among consumers, which often helps to increase sales. Instead of fighting each other, environmental activists and business leaders are finding a way to work together to protect the rain forests and other environmentally sensitive areas.

Christopher M. Wille, "Certification: A Catalyst for Partnerships," *Human Ecology Review,* vol. 11, 2004, pp. 288–91. Copyright © 2004 by the Society for Human Ecology. Reproduced by permission of Copyright Clearance Center, Inc.

B usiness and conservation leaders have circled each other during the past decade or so in a wary dance often punctuated by missteps and misunderstanding. NGOs [nongovernmental organizations] and companies have experimented with joint councils, codes of conducts, licensing agreements and other overtures with mixed success. Even though they often share common objectives, there are several inherent impediments to accord between activists and capitalists, including communication barriers hardened by different worldviews, widely different operational styles, a lack of trust and different priorities.

Some NGOs, almost accidentally, discovered a way to get past the barriers: admit that business and development is necessary, set guidelines for ethical and/or environmentally sound business practices, develop independent monitoring systems and create motivations for responsible practices, including economic incentives. This cohort of activities, collectively called certification, is increasingly seen as a way to bring business and activists together around the same table and same objectives.

Certification programs have been developed for a range of enterprises, including agriculture, forestry, fisheries and manufacturing. Among the best known are the organic and Fair Trade movements in agriculture, Social Accountability International, Rainforest Alliance Certified and the Ethical Trade Initiative. There is even a sector association called the International Social and Environmental Accreditation and Labeling Alliance (ISEAL).

The Beginning of Cooperation

When the Rainforest Alliance was launched in 1987, the "corporate responsibility" movement, now in full cry, was still being hopefully heralded in journals . . . with scant evidence that it would ever be realized. There was no reason to think that a small group of activists coming together in New York City to decry the destruction of distant rainforests would eventually form partnerships with some of the same companies it was protesting or that businesses would ever welcome NGO guidance and oversight.

At that time, environmental activists and captains of industry were equally mired in habits long acquired, both acting (if at all) reflexively rather than with thoughtful reflection. The Rainforest Alliance was urged by critics of capitalism to lead or join boycotts against products coming from tropical areas. Alliance members knew that boycotts could call attention to a problem, but rarely solve it. Protesting imports of tropical hardwoods, rainforest beef, coffee or bananas would not save wildlife habitats nor help the millions in developing countries who produce these commodities.

Setting Standards

As one of its first moves, the Alliance called together a brain trust of foresters, timber company executives, scientists, loggers, environmentalists and other stakeholders to debate alternatives to reckless and accelerating deforestation. From these meetings emerged the idea of setting standards for responsible forest management, urging timber companies to adopt prudent practices, and then rewarding the best performers with a green seal of approval. Instead of castigating an entire industry, the Alliance determined to seek out the progressive practitioners, incite awareness, raise the bar of acceptable practices, and bring consumer power to bear. This was the opposite of a boycott; a buycott.

> *Protesting imports of tropical hardwoods, rainforest beef, coffee or bananas would not save wildlife habitats nor help the millions in developing countries who produce these commodities.*

In 1990, Alliance operatives in Costa Rica joined with other NGOs to denounce the multinational banana companies, which were deforesting, littering the landscape with plastic and organic wastes, polluting streams, using unholy amounts of pesticides and neglecting the rights and welfare of workers. Costa Rica was at that time and remains the second largest banana exporter, after Ecuador. Banana production, which had been an economic mainstay in Costa Rica for a century, was the leading source of foreign exchange and the largest private-sector employer.

Following the model used with the timber industry, the Alliance organized a two-year-long series of meetings among banana farmers, NGOs, government agencies, community leaders and others. It took months to break down the initial hostilities that had built up between greens and bananeros. The workshops were brokered by scientists and conservationists who spoke a cool, neutral language based on observable facts, kept the discussions as free as possible of accusation and focused on the practical and possible remedies. Eventually, agreements began to emerge about what constitutes responsible plantation management.

Banana Companies Improve
Their Business Practices

This consensus was fashioned into nine principles that embrace: conservation of ecosystems, water, soil and wildlife; fair treatment for workers and demonstrated commitment to their rights as guaranteed under the International Labour Organization conventions and national laws; a good-neighbor policy with local communities; integrated crop management to control and reduce agrochemical use; policies to manage, reduce, reuse and recycle all wastes; and a planning and monitoring system on each farm that can ensure continual improvements.

Sustainability . . . is defined as three interlocking circles: social responsibility, economic viability and environmental protection.

Concrete and measurable indicators that permitted trained auditors to evaluate and score a farm point by point bolstered the nine principles. The indicators provide enough detail to guide the development and implementation of best management practices. As examples, there are indicators for the kinds of trees that must be planted, which agrochemicals are permitted, the width of the required buffer strips along streams, the disposal of wastes, the content of worker contracts, the construction of sanitary facilities, workplace safety, wages, training, health care, and wastewater treatment.

As with forestry, the Rainforest Alliance collaborated with other NGOs in developing a certification system that gave farmers direction and incentive to adopt the more responsible practices. Family owned banana farms and Chiquita began experimenting with the standards while the Rainforest Alliance trained agronomists, biologists, sociologists and other specialists to be farm auditors. Independent farms in Hawaii and Costa Rica were the first to comply with the standards and win certification in 1993. The next year, two Chiquita farms were certified in Costa Rica, and the company made a commitment to certify all its farms in the country, and later, the region.

The Chiquita Turnaround

Chiquita, long the trendsetter in the banana business, invested eight years and an estimated $22 million in bringing all the company farms up to the standards. While this was challenge enough, the company also developed a code of core values and trained all employees in them, began a series of corporate responsibility reports praised for their candor and comprehensiveness, made a landmark agreement with the global farmworkers union, and began adopting a second certification program for labor issues, SA8000, managed by Social Accountability International.

"Chiquita has brought an entirely new dimension to the concept of a responsible company," say J. Gary Taylor and Patricia Scharlin, authors of a new book about the Rainforest Alliance and Chiquita partnership, *Smart Alliance—How a Global Corporation and Environmental Activists Transformed a Tarnished Brand.* The story of the Chiquita turn-around is a favored example in corporate responsibility conferences because the company converted from a closed compound to an open, transparent, progressive enterprise willing to listen to critics and cooperate with stakeholders. As one journalist wrote, "from pariah to paragon."

Sustainable Development

Few businesses were ever charmed by the commonsense of conservation, the prudent precept defined by [founding father of wildlife ecology] Aldo Leopold as using resources wisely today so that the next generation will have options for development as well as functioning ecosystems and the inspiration of nature's beauty and mystery. In the 1990s, the term *sustainable development* came into vogue. Even though the intent of sustainable development was nearly identical to *conservation*, business soon adopted it, in part because they could define it to their liking.

Sustainability, like conservation, is defined as three interlocking circles: social responsibility, economic viability and environmental protection. In order to pursue sustainability the

Rainforest Alliance's certification programs address all three sectors at once, and this holistic, integrated approach makes sense to progressive business leaders.

With globalization came seismic shifts in the relative power of the traditional actors in the long battle between environmentalism and capitalism, unfolding realizations on both sides of the values and roles of the other, new allies to both sides, more exposure for companies and better communications closing conventional information gaps.

During the 1990s, conservation groups began to comprehend the amount of power concentrated in a few companies. Some companies are wealthier than many countries, and in any case, governments in tropical countries—even those not debilitated by corruption—have their hands full trying to provide basic services and rights to exploding populations. Governments dependent on exports are timid regulators of exporting companies, especially large, multinational companies that can take their business elsewhere. Legislation and enforcement rarely function with enough speed, efficiency and stakeholder buy-in to deal effectively with environmental issues that gather velocity and complexity at breakneck rates.

Growing Power of NGOs

The Rainforest Alliance is managing a new program in Mexico and Central America, bringing together alliances between responsible producers of bananas, coffee and timber with responsible buyers. In addition to Chiquita, a number of coffee companies are participating, led by Kraft, which is buying unprecedented amounts of certified sustainable beans and inculcating sustainability into the company philosophy as well as its supply chain. Procter & Gamble, another of the world's largest coffee roasters, is also selling a certified sustainable coffee under its gourmet brand, Millstone. Among the timber producing and wood buying companies participating: Home Depot, Ikea, Dixon Ticonderoga, Potlatch, Tembec and Domtar.

Certification, international conventions such as the Global Compact, the Internet stockholder interventions and other tools have given NGOs more traction in dealing with companies. NGOs can attack or partner with a company in one place and affect its holdings worldwide. Authors Taylor and Scharlin add, "Multinational companies, for their part, have no choice but to engage globally. Most no longer boast of the national origins of their products; instead, they rely increasingly on global brand names and polished corporate images, making them increasingly vulnerable to the rancor and ridicule of NGO campaigns. The walls between campaigners and corporations began to crumble in the 1990s."

Urging Corporate Responsibility

NGOs and activists have long demanded that business managers show a greater sense of social and environmental responsibility. "But it's increasingly clear that the calls are coming from mainstream quarters of society as well," says Roger L. Martin of the Rotman School of Management in Ontario, Canada. "Many consumers and investors, as well as a growing number of business leaders, have added their voices to those urging corporations to remember their obligations to their employees, their communities, and the environment, even as they pursue profits for shareholders." Martin published an analytical tool in the *Harvard Business Review* to help business executives "calculate the return on corporate responsibility." Martin called this tool "the virtue matrix."

Mid-career business professionals from Columbia University's Center for Environmental Research and Conservation conducted a study for the Rainforest Alliance to evaluate the financial benefits of engaging in sustainable business practices. Through analysis of some of the Rainforest Alliance partnerships with companies, the investigators identified the following potential benefits:

- Improved corporate reputation and positive brand impact
- Strong corporate governance
- Improved regulatory relationships
- Risk mitigation and management
  - Crisis avoidance
  - Defense of existing markets
  - Reduced risk of business disruption
- Managing food safety risks
- Competitive advantage
- Access to new markets
- Cost reductions
  - Reduced employee turnover
  - Lower chemical application costs/lower risk associated with chemical use

    ◦ Savings realized through reductions in water and electricity use and implementation of recycling programs
    ◦ Lower insurance premiums
    ◦ Reduced cost of capital

While researchers note that only some of these benefits generate quantifiable and immediate financial benefits, investors and managers are now beginning to look at the long-term impact on financial performance. Piet Sprengers, director of a green investment group in The Netherlands called VBDO, says that while many investors are interested in using their shares as leverage to change corporate behavior, increasingly investors are looking at a company's social performance as an indicator of its projected, long-range performance. VBDO is sponsoring studies of the impacts of Dutch companies on the environment, especially on biodiversity. Conservationists are finding new allies and stakeholders to support their traditional work: shareholders. As an example, the Rainforest Alliance collaborates with VBDO in a study of the impacts of rapidly expanding soy production in Brazil.

Activist Groups Partner with Companies

The growing prominence of the *concept* of partnership is helping bridge activist groups and companies. David F. Murphy and Gill Coleman of the New Academy of Business in the United Kingdom, write: "Partnership is an idea with increasing political power today, in the sense that it invokes positive connotations within society which make people act in novel ways."

The Rainforest Alliance entered partnerships through the side door of certification and the application of a green seal of approval. With 17 years of experience, Use Alliance can show that certification is a powerful magnetic force that draws together companies and NGOs that share similar objectives. The process of coming together to set standards, providing incentives to producers and companies to meet those standards, and then independently verifying performance allows diverse actors to merge their economic, ethical and environmental interests. In addition to embracing the Three Es of sustainability, the certification process stimulates and monitors another essential ingredient of progress: continuous change.

The Alliance and other NGOs leading certification programs have learned valuable lessons that help smooth the way for partnerships with industry, including:

- The importance of building and maintaining trust through honest dialogue and crystalline transparency;
- The need to define the political ecology surrounding any particular industry so that sister NGOs and other stakeholders are in sync with any potential partnership;
- The need to build expertise in the target industry, understand the economics as well as the ethical and environmental issues, and be fluent in its language and attuned to its rhythms;
- The need to guard NGO independence and green seal credibility;
- The importance of clarity and agreed rules in marketing and messaging so that companies can take credit and profits from the relationship while maintaining its credibility;
- Prove that responsible business is smart business.

The public-private-partnership movement, although at least 30 years old, is still finding its feet. There have been some successes and many learning experiences. But with the decline in nation-state regulatory power, increasing demands for business to be more accountable amidst almost routine corporate scandals, and the growing reach and power of civil society groups, stakeholder and stockholders, there is little doubt that partnerships will continue to shine a light forward in the quest for sustainability.

9

Environmentalists Who Work with Corporations Harm Rain Forest Communities

Aziz Choudry

Aziz Choudry is an environmental activist, researcher, and writer.

When large corporations send researchers into the rain forest to search for potential pharmaceutical and agricultural products that could be developed from plants and insects, it is called bioprospecting. To the indigenous people who live in the rain forest, it is often seen as piracy, or biopiracy. Multinational corporations such as Exxon, Monsanto, and Bristol Myers Squibb, under the guise of a supposed environmental organization called Conservation International (CI), are exploiting the natural wealth of the rain forests and giving little in return. Other members of CI fight to evict indigenous people from their lands in order to gain easier access to the valuable resources of the rain forests. While putting an environmentally friendly face on its activities, Conservation International is actually acting to further the agenda of big business at the expense of tropical forests and impoverished natives and their communities.

I ts website proclaims: "A passionate few can make the difference in the world." [Former secretary of state] Colin Powell

Aziz Choudry, "Raiders of the Lost Biosphere: Conservation International," *Earth First!*, vol. 24, April 30, 2004, p. 10. Copyright © 2004 by Daily Planet Publishing. Reproduced by permission.

says that its work is "amazing." Its president, Russell Mitter-meier, confesses to a lifelong Tarzan fixation, while its vice-chair [Harrison Ford] is the actor who played Indiana Jones. In 2001, it received what the media dubbed the largest grant to an environmental organization—$261 million spread over 10 years.

> ***CI's track record suggests a motivation to conserve natural areas as a resource for bioprospecting rather than out of concern for the rights of the people who have . . . protected these ecosystems for so long.*"

The organization is Conservation International (CI). Founded in 1987, with headquarters in Washington, DC, CI's stated mission is "to conserve the Earth's living natural heritage, our global biodiversity and to demonstrate that human societies are able to live harmoniously with nature." It operates in more than 30 countries—in the Americas, Asia, Africa and the Pacific. But like Harrison Ford, CI does a lot of acting, applying copious layers of green makeup. Unfortunately, for many indigenous peoples affected by CI's brand of "conservation," this is no movie set.

It is no coincidence that indigenous people live in the world's remaining biologically diverse regions. Yet CI frequently depicts them as threats to the environment, accusing them of illegal logging, overpopulation and slash-and-burn agriculture. Leave it to the experts to save these places, says CI, through "applying innovations in science, economics and policy."

CI's major supporters include Cemex, Citigroup, Chiquita, ExxonMobil Foundation, Ford, Gap, JP Morgan Chase and Co., McDonald's, Sony, Starbucks, United Airlines and Disney. Gordon Moore, CI's executive committee chair—and donor of the $261 million grant—founded the Intel Corporation. CI claims that its corporate supporters "share a common concern about protecting the environment."

Taking Advantage of the Locals

CI uses its considerable financial resources, political influence and environmental sweet talk to quietly access, administer and purchase biologically diverse areas throughout the world, which it puts at the disposal of multinational corporations. CI's track record suggests a motivation to conserve natural areas as a resource for bioprospecting rather than out of concern for the rights of the people who have lived with and protected these ecosystems for so long.

In 1997, CI signed a comprehensive bioprospecting agreement with California-based Hyseq, which specializes in genomic sequencing. CI agreed to test flora and fauna samples for possible drug candidates and to provide regular reports on its findings to Hyseq. In addition to an initial contribution, Hyseq pays CI on both a per-country basis and an annual fee. Hyseq is also free to pursue intellectual property claims over any results.

In Panama, CI has worked with Novartis, Monsanto and others in "ecologically guided bioprospecting"—seeking pharmaceutical and agricultural products from plants, fungi and insects. In Surinam, CI cooperated with Bristol Myers Squibb's ethnobotanists in collecting plant samples. It was here that CI worked to win the trust of indigenous communities and healers in order to negotiate a very dubious "benefit-sharing" agreement.

> *In the name of environmental protection, CI is pitting indigenous communities against each other, raising fears of conflict in an area that is already heavily militarized.*

Half a world away, in the Solomon Islands, CI runs a project that sees local people harvesting the Ngali nut. CI claims that this provides a viable economic alternative to logging the country's tropical forests. The project supplies the operations of an Australian entrepreneur, Peter Hull.

On May 28, 2002, Hull was granted a patent by the US Patent Office for use of the nut oil in the "treatment of arthritis and other similar conditions." He is applying for patents in 127 countries. Hull says that he works with CI to convince village elders "that it is in their best interests to preserve and protect their rainforest, in order to harvest the Ngali nuts from it."

While Hull can earn an estimated $10,000 dollars for each kilogram of nut oil, last year [2003], the World Bank put per capita income in the Solomons at $570. This seems to be yet another example of a CI collaboration that supports the rights of private companies to cash in on traditional knowledge and patent lifeforms. The locals—pardon the pun—get peanuts.

Exploitation in Chiapas

CI's involvement in the [rainforest of] Selva Lacandona, Chiapas, is also deeply disturbing. Through a 1991 debt-for-nature swap, CI bought the right to set up a genetic research station in the Montes Azules Biosphere reserve.

It currently is urging the Mexican government to evict the indigenous communities in Montes Azules, accusing them of destroying the rainforest. And in the name of environmental protection, CI is pitting indigenous communities against each other, raising fears of conflict in an area that is already heavily militarized.

The giant Mexican agribusiness corporation, Grupo Pulsar, works closely with CI in Mexico. Between 1996 and 2000, it donated $10 million to CI-Mexico.

Pulsar's claimed concern for ecology and biodiversity does not extend to its main activities, which include the promotion of monoculture in Chiapas and the planned planting of more than 700,000 acres of non-native eucalyptus trees.

The Chiapas-based Center of Economic and Political Research for Community Action believes that the Pulsar Group's donations could more likely be a remuneration for CI bioprospecting within the Selva Lacandona.

> *CI believes that the best way to conserve biodiversity is to privatize it.*

Pulsar has the technology, the resources and the business knowledge to know that there are large rewards awaiting the "discovery" of medicinal properties extracted from the Lacandona. CI "facilitates" the Pulsar Group's entrance, and it helps orient technicians in the prospecting while projecting a conservation facade to the world.

The World Bank–backed Meso-American Biological Corridor project is also supported by CI. Many indigenous communities, social movements and environmental organizations have condemned this project as an attempt to greenwash the massive Plan Puebla Panama infrastructure scheme and as a front for corporate biopiracy in the region.

Gross Disrespect

In many countries, the establishment of CI-initiated protected areas have trampled on indigenous peoples' land, social, spiritual, cultural, political and economic rights, without consultation, in deals cut with governments and corporations in the name of "conservation." The Wai Wai and Wapishana in southern Guyana recently accused CI of "gross disrespect" toward indigenous peoples in its move to set up a protected area on their territories.

Given the significant involvement of mining, oil and gas corporations in CI's program it is sobering to note that many of its "biodiversity hotspots" and project operations are on or adjacent to sites of oil, gas and mineral exploration and extraction —Chiapas, Palawan (Philippines), Colombia, West Papua, Aceh (Indonesia) and Papua New Guinea. Indigenous peoples continue to resist the corporate assaults on their territories, while CI actively champions the causes of these multinational corporations to be seen as environmentally and socially responsible.

In September 2002, mining giant Rio Tinto launched a partnership with CI in southeastern Guinea's Pic De Fon, giving support for a rapid assessment program of the rich biodiversity in a forest area where Rio Tinto was exploring (it has diamond and iron ore operations in Guinea).

Rio Tinto's environmental policy adviser Tom Burke sits on the advisory board for CI's Center for Environmental Leadership in Business (CELB), along with executives from International Paper, Starbucks and British Petroleum.

Another CI project is the Energy and Biodiversity Initiative (EBI). Convened by the CELB, participants include British Petroleum, Chevron Texaco, Fauna & Flora International, Shell, Smithsonian Institution, Statoil, The Nature Conservancy and IUCN—The World Conservation Union. Last August [2003], the EBI released a report, "Energy and Biodiversity: Integrating Biodiversity Conservation into Oil and Gas Development."

Given its corporate nature and its "partnerships," it is easy to see why CI is so uncritical about the impact of economic injustice on the environment and biodiversity. Indeed, it proposes market "solutions" to address environmental destruction that has been caused or exacerbated by free market capitalism.

CI believes that the best way to conserve biodiversity is to privatize it. Yet those who are paying attention to CI's activities see this approach leading to tropical forests becoming "corporate-administered genetic colonies."

In the struggles for social and ecological justice, and against corporate colonialism, it is very clear which side Conservation International is on. Not ours.

10

Ecotourism Can Help Save the Rain Forest

Keith Wilson

Keith Wilson is a photographer and travel writer whose work appears in Outdoor Photography, Geographical, *and other publications.*

In Malaysian Borneo thousands of rural poor people are cutting down the rain forest in order to plant rice. While these families eke out a meager living, others have discovered the value of preserving the forest for ecotourism. As growing numbers of westerners travel to places like Borneo to take jungle treks and learn about rain forest wildlife, locals catering to the ecotourism trade have learned that they can earn much more money by preserving their lands than clearing them for farming. This grassroots conservation not only brings benefits to indigenous people but also allows travelers from industrial nations to learn about the environmental value of rain forests. Working together, ecotourists and their guides hold the promise of survival for threatened rain forest ecosystems.

Early October in Sabah, northern Borneo. The wet season is just a few weeks away. On a trail winding across the steep foothills of Mount Kinabalu, I stop to wipe my eyes, which are stinging from the perspiration that runs persistently down my brow. The humidity is unlikely anything I've experienced before, but my guide is eager to make up for lost time and reach our campsite in time for lunch. As I reach for my camera to photograph the distant, hazy rainforest, a small bare-footed woman of about 60, carrying a loaded basket on her back and wielding a machete, marches effortlessly past my perspiring frame, slashing at ferns and grasses along the way.

"Who was that?" I ask my guide in breathless admiration.

"My mother," he answers.

By the time I've recovered my composure, she has rounded the next bend and vanished from sight. I wipe my brow again and follow.

I'm heading for the Kiau Spur of 4,095-metre Mount Kinabalu, Southeast Asia's highest peak. My guide is Sardib Miki, 35, a former trekking porter who has climbed Kinabalu more than 1,000 times. Miki now owns a small slice of rainforest that represents one of Malaysia's more successful examples of grassroots conservation.

These foothills may be steep, but over the years local farmers have used slash-and-burn techniques to clear the forest, build narrow terraces and plant rice. Although the majority of their plots occupy only a few hectares, together they strip the rainforest as effectively as any illegal logger.

The farmers use a crude irrigation network of bamboo pipes to divert water from the many streams to their rice crops. Every few hundred metres we pass makeshift huts about half the size of a London suburban front room, where the farmers shelter from the sun and tropical downpours. Although they occasionally sleep here, their homes are in the village of Kampung Kiau Nuluh (Kiau), to where the rice will be transported after the harvest. This is subsistence farming to feed a rapidly growing population and each year another slice of Borneo's tropical rainforest is razed and rice planted in its place.

> *Each year another slice of Borneo's tropical rainforest is razed and rice planted in its place.*

Suddenly, the landscape changes. Ahead of us, the path disappears into a green wall of dense shadows, giant ferns and towering lichen-covered trees. It's a relief to be out of the sun and within the cool confines of this arboreal world, but there is still no time to stop.

After crossing two rivers and slipping repeatedly on steep, mud-covered trails, I'm eventually confronted by a sign rising from the jungle floor: 'Miki Survival Camp'. There's even a website address at the bottom of this rather incongruous notice. The camp is in a small clearing along with two semi-permanent shelters built of bamboo and forest timbers. It forms the heart of Miki's small private holding of pristine rainforest, located just a couple of hours' walk from the boundary of Kinabalu National Park.

The camp exists because Miki chose not to follow his neighbours' example of tearing up the forest to plant rice. Instead, he realised a much better living could be made by saving his trees and cashing in on Malaysia's expanding ecotourism industry. Nearly five years on, he has led groups of travellers, mostly from the UK, on jungle treks, teaching them how to live off the land and introducing them to some of the hundreds of species of rare tropical plants. But this wasn't his original plan. Because three mountain rivers flow through his land, Miki initially entertained the idea of clearing the forest to build freshwater ponds for commercial fish farming.

Marketing Jungle Treks

Miki seems shy and quiet. But his slight build and limited English hide a level of commitment matched only by his amazing stamina. As a mountain runner he twice finished in the top five of the Mount Kinabalu International Climbathon. He has also represented Malaysia in the World Mountain Running Trophy. Success in these races earned him enough money to build a house in Kiau, home to his wife and four children. It's from this house that the jungle excursions begin and end. Nearly 100 groups have so far enjoyed his hospitality.

So what happened to make Miki choose conservation over fish farming? In 1998, while working for Tham Yau Kong, one of Sabah's leading tour operators, Miki led a group of tourists on a jungle trek in Long Pasia, eastern Sabah. Unfortunately, this area of rainforest was blighted by loggers, something the tourists found distressing. This got him thinking about the potential of his own land. "I thought my forest was good enough for jungle treks as there was no logging, and it was closer to Kinabalu too," Miki recalls.

With Tham's help, he set up Miki Jungle Survival and marketed the treks in the UK through a Borneo travel specialist. The combination of climbing Mount Kinabalu and exploring the unique environment of a tropical rainforest has proven irresistible to many. Although Miki has taken hundreds of trekkers to the top of Kinabalu as a registered mountain guide since 1989, his primary concern now is to preserve this patch of rainforest and encourage other landholders in Kiau to follow his lead by using ecotourism to make a living out of the jungle. So far he has persuaded more than 40 others not to fell their trees. As a result, more than 40 hectares of rainforest along the border of the national park have been saved.

During my brief foray into Miki's domain, he introduced me to some of the forest's edible fruits and plants: wild mango, runtuh, lychee, rambutan and durian. Of course, these are well known to most Western palates, but even in the 21st century, new species are being discovered. For example, *Begonia chongii*, a new herb, was found near Miki's forest in April 2001. This part of Sabah has a historical connection with the great Victorian plant collectors—it was through these dense forests that Sir Hugh Low, the first man to reach the summit of Kinabalu, travelled in the early 1850s.

The fauna is harder to see in this damp and dark environment, but Miki reels off an impressive list of animals that live here: macque monkeys, mouse deer, orang-utan, clouded leopard. . . . My ears prick up at this point. This last animal is nocturnal, rarely seen and one of the world's most endangered big cats.

"Have you ever seen one?" I ask.

"No, but I have seen footprints coming down from there," replies Miki pointing in the direction of Kinabalu. My father saw one a long time ago."

> **❝** Miki . . . realised a much better living could be made by saving his trees and cashing in on Malaysia's expanding ecotourism industry. **❞**

While we talk, Miki's brother Yanis prepares the lunchtime noodles in a black pot on the fire. The smoke hangs over the campsite before drifting past a sign inscribed "Canford" that hangs from the roof of the larger of the two shelters. It was built with funds raised by students of Canford School in Dorset, who stayed at Miki Survival Camp in July 2001. The 13 A-level students, who also reached the summit of Kinabalu, were so impressed by their rainforest experience that they decided to give something back and raised £500 [about $950] for the construction of the 20 man shelter. "It's solidly built and won't need replacing for about five years," says an appreciative Miki. Normally, they need replacing every six to 12 months, so the Canford shelter has contributed in its own way to conserving the rainforest by saving on materials.

Inspiring Others

After my visit, I meet with Canford School's biology teacher Robert Hooker. "It's nice to see that people are trying to hold on to the forests now because it's so important," he says. "There's so much to learn, so much more to discover. There's a lot of diversity packed into a small place." The students have posted more than 300 photographs from their Borneo trip on the school website. However, hopes of bringing another party of A-level scholars to Miki Survival Camp haven't materialised since the terrorist attacks in the USA [in 2001] and Bali [in 2002].

However, despite the impact of global terrorism, of greater long-term importance to the conservation of the rainforest is Miki's mission to persuade more villagers to make a living from ecotourism. His mentor, Tham Yau Kong, is unequivocal about the significance of Miki Survival Camp. "This is the best example of genuine private conservation," he says. "He has managed to save 40 hectares as others have been inspired to join him."

Of course, asking villagers to swap their hoes for a backpack makes economic sense, but making the argument isn't difficult when each week lines of Western tourists pass through the rice terraces to Miki Survival Camp. On our way out of the forest and back onto the scrubby slopes of sprouting rice, Miki points to one of the smaller holdings, barely a hectare in size. "A hectare of hill rice will make about 2,500 ringgit [£500] a year," he tells me. "You can only plant once every five years to keep the soil productive." During that same period, Miki says, he's made many times that figure from each hectare of his rainforest. With the money he's made, he's been able to extend his house, buy a van and take advantage of the recently installed electricity supply by adding a television and refrigerator.

Miki's faith in ecotourism isn't just based on the changes it's brought to his life. He also sees the preservation of the rainforest as vital to the future of his local community. "The forest isn't just for tourism," he says. "Most of the things we need are in this area. I believe our children will find more medicinal plants and more edible plants. It is important, too, that the upper slopes aren't cleared, otherwise water for our village will dry up."

Ultimately, conservation is about keeping the basic commodities of life, for life. Fortunately, in the remote jungles of northern Borneo that lesson is hitting home, thanks to a diminutive mountain porter named Miki.

11

Ecotourism Harms the Rain Forest

Gregory C. Jones

Gregory C. Jones has a master of environmental management degree from Yale's School of Forestry and Environmental Studies, and lives in Calgary, Canada.

The Inca Trail is the name of a twenty-five-mile-long walking route that leads to the ancient Inca city of Machu Picchu in Peru. Although it takes the average tourist four to five days of strenuous hiking to reach the dramatic mountaintop ruins high in the Amazon rain forest, nearly eighty thousand make the trek every year. The impact of these large groups of people and porters is threatening this delicate landscape. Hikers leave behind massive piles of trash and human waste, and the sheer number of people walking on the trail is causing serious erosion. While ecotourism has helped the local economy, it has also led to the pollution of the drinking water that natives rely on and upsets the ecological balance of this endangered region. Hikers need to learn to explore the trail without damaging it.

O n a bright July morning, I climbed the worn stone steps to Warmiwanusca, or Dead Woman's Pass. At 4200 metres [13,779 feet above sea level], Warmiwanusca is the highest point along the Inca Trail leading to the fabled citadel of Machu Picchu in the Peruvian Andes. Standing atop the pass, I could see waterfalls pouring from shining granite peaks, con-

Gregory C. Jones, "The New Conquistadors: Trekkers on the Inca Trail Threaten a Priceless Landscape," *Alternatives Journal: Canadian Environmental Ideas and Action,* vol. 27, Fall 2001, p. 7. Copyright © 2001 by Alternatives, Inc. Annual subscriptions (6/yr.) $35 (plus GST) from *Alternatives Journal,* Faculty of Environmental Studies, University of Waterloo, Waterloo, Ontario N2L 3G1 Canada; www.alternatives journal.ca. Reproduced by permission of the publisher and the author.

dors circling over wild puna grasslands, and clouds of mist rising from moss-covered forests. Lost in my solitary thoughts, I could forget—for a minute—that I was far from alone.

All around me, covering most of the pass, hundreds of other people were resting in the sunshine: tourists, porters and guides. And it was only nine in the morning. Others were on their way.

In recent years, the trail has become the most heavily used trekking route in South America. In 1990, 8000 people hiked the trail; by 1999 the number had exploded to 77,000 [and has remained about the same in the subsequent years].

The trail runs through the Machu Picchu Historical Sanctuary, which, at 340 square kilometres [11 square miles], is less than half the area of New York City and 1/20 of the area of Banff National Park [in Canada]. Perched on the eastern rim of the Andes, where steep-sided mountains are engulfed by the green of the Amazon rain forest, the sanctuary is centred around the Machu Picchu Citadel—one of the most famous archaeological sites on the planet. It is also home to a magnificent variety of plants and animals occupying habitats from dripping cloud forest to dry alpine puna grasslands, including an estimated 400 species of orchids and the endangered spectacled bear.

The mystical experiences that so many are seeking in this rich environment are often lost in the stampede. But more troublesome than the crowds themselves are the effects that trekkers are inflicting on all of the cultural and biological wonders that have drawn people here in the first place. Today, if you leave the Inca Trail and peak over a hill here, or through the forest there, you may see not a mist-enshrouded ruin or a cluster of rare orchids, but over-flowing pits of garbage and mounds of dirty toilet paper.

Garbage is not something new on the trail. Plastic, tin and glass have been accumulating in some campsite garbage pits for over 30 years. But other problems, like soil erosion and lack of sanitary facilities, have been neglected as well, and the problems are mounting.

The Effects of Ecotourism

Surprisingly, despite the fame of Machu Picchu and the Inca Trail and their enormous historical, cultural and economic imtance to Peru, no study had been attempted to monitor and assess how tourism is affecting these sites and their natural surroundings—until now.

With financing from the government of Finland, a new agency was formed in 1995 to foster solutions to the mounting problems in the sanctuary. The agency, named Programa Machu Picchu, kick-starts research, funds education programs, and buys equipment to assist the local community and underfunded sanctuary personnel. In 1999, I was asked by Programa to investigate the issue of the environmental impact of tourism on the Inca Trail. As an environmental biologist and an avid trekker, I leapt at the chance.

> *If you leave the Inca Trail . . . you may see not a mist-enshrouded ruin or a cluster of rare orchids, but over-flowing pits of garbage and mounds of dirty toilet paper.*

Within a few days of my arrival in Peru, I made my first visit to the most heavily impacted and controversial place along the Inca Trail—Winay Wayna camp. Winay Wayna, meaning forever young, is the lyrical name given originally by archaelogists to the adjacent Inca Ruins and adopted by the camp. But the campsite has become ground zero in an undeclared war between the trail's pro-development and environmentalist factions, and here development is firmly entrenched in the form of stores, a hotel and a restaurant.

As I approached, I discovered that the steep, treacherous trail descending the last half-mile to the camp is deteriorating rapidly. After decades of heavy use, the trail is a gully through which a river of water pours in the rainy season. Old stone steps lie at odd angles. Loose rocks along the trail await the unwary, overburdened, tired traveler.

Winay Wayna itself evokes many emotions. Some visitors see the restaurant, hotel, hot showers and flush toilets as a blessing: the first chance to be clean and comfortable in three days. And the location is spectacular: two ancient Inca ruins flank the site, their terraces sweeping across the mountainside. The rushing Urubamba River is a blue-white ribbon far below, and high Andean subtropical forests march up the opposite side of the river valley.

Others, however, see the camp as over-developed, crowded and inhospitable. In the July-to-September high season, the cavernous warehouse-style restaurant is usually packed, filled with a deafening din, and stinking heavily of sweat and spilled beer. On some days, every square inch of flat land in the camp is claimed by early afternoon. One night in July, 80 school children had no place to go, and slept in a jumbled mass in the campsite workers' kitchen. The camp running water, arriving from springs higher on the mountain, occasionally runs dry in the high tourist season. The camp terraces are becoming scarred and rutted from heavy use.

The message is clear: Winay Wayna is forever young in name only.

My second trip to the Inca Trail began two weeks later and 25 kilometres away, at the railroad stop where most visitors begin their trek. Considering that this is the trailhead of South America's most famous trail, it is remarkably nondescript. No visitor centre offers advice, and no sign points the way. Alongside a rusty brown rail car that has been removed from the tracks, tickets are sold from a tiny green hut.

The only information dispensed by park workers here is a small pamphlet with a map of the trail—so it is not surprising that few visitors know of the regulations and minimum-impact principles that park managers would like to see followed. Even the mantra of "pack it in, pack it out," which is standard trekkers' practice just about everywhere, is largely ignored here. As I walked from the trailhead to the small village of Wayflabamba, I counted one piece of garbage for every six steps that I took.

> *At a small trailside camp . . . pipes carry the wastewater out of the toilets and into the forest—just out of view—and drop it.*

Garbage on the Inca Trail is a big issue. Park workers have installed waste bins along the route, trying to reduce indiscriminate littering along the trail. However, their well-meaning effort has given trail users the impression that the sanctuary has some sort of well-thought-out disposal system, negating the need for people to pack out their garbage. Most trail users happily use these bins. Few know that the garbage in these bins never leaves the sanctuary.

Behind every bin there is a dump-pit, just out of sight. Park workers wait until the tourists have passed and then empty the bins into the pits. Most of these pits are overflowing, spilling plastic bottles and tin cans into sanctuary grasslands and forests. Park personnel cannot excavate new pits fast enough to capture all the garbage that accumulates during the high season.

From Wayflabamba, the trail begins to wind upward through cool, wet forests and high, grassy alpine slopes. Part of the attraction of the trail is the variety of experiences it can provide. Some sections are of stone and others are hard-packed earth. Local villagers still travel along some sections with horses and cattle, while other parts see only tourists and their guides. Some sections meander along valley bottoms, while others lead up steep, imposing stairways.

Human Sewage and Invasive Plants

Over the course of three months, I established study sites in each of these areas to document garbage, erosion, side-trails and other patterns of damage caused by tourism. All of these are relatively typical impacts along recreational trails, but what concerned me most as I continued towards Machu Picchu was something else—human sewage.

Many Programa researchers say sewage is a larger issue than garbage because of the threat of spreading disease, in addition to serious aesthetic impacts. On the Inca Trail most bathrooms don't have septic tanks. Some don't even have pits. At a small trailside camp called Chaquicocha, for example, pipes carry the wastewater out of the toilets and into the forest—just out of view—and drop it. The water flows down the slope and away from camp, but into the creek below.

Creeks contaminated in this way immediately become a threat to the health of hikers, porters, and local residents downstream, especially those who don't have the resources to purify the water before they drink it. So it has become common for porters to beg for water from iodine-equipped tourists to avoid drinking from the polluted streams.

Another impact—and perhaps the greatest threat to the ecological balance of the sanctuary—comes from invasive exotic plant and animal species that have been spread by tourists and local farmers. Kikuyu, a grass species from Africa, now covers the ground at almost every archaeological site in the area. Archaeologists say that the roots of the grass pry Inca stonework apart, causing terraces and buildings to collapse. Kikuyu's spread is also evicting native grasses and a variety of other local species, including the sanctuary's famous orchids.

> **❝ The trail and the sanctuary must be protected without threatening local livelihoods. ❞**

Melinis minutiflora, Molasses grass, is another African species that has been spreading along the trail and into the Machu Picchu Citadel. This species is of even greater concern because it is very susceptible to fire. In the past decade, tourists have caused several wildfires. In 1994, an untended campfire at Phuyu Pata Marca camp, three kilometres [1.8 miles] up the trail from Winay Wayna, spread to grass and then to forest, burning thousands of hectares.

Biologist Julio Ochoa, who has worked in the sanctuary for over a decade, notes that the more often fires occur, the more forest and native grassland is replaced by Molasses grass—creating a vicious cycle that increases the risk of future fires and changes the ecology of the sanctuary forever.

Researchers at Programa Machu Picchu are well aware of the garbage, the human waste, the soil erosion, the invasive species, and the fires. But they also know that the trail and the sanctuary must be protected without threatening local livelihoods. In the last year [2000], Programa has completed fire prevention and waste management plans for the sanctuary, and Inca Trail managers have recently established new rules that will attack two key problems on the trail: overcrowding and littering. In early 2001, sanctuary managers increased admission charges from $26 to $70, established a pack-it-in pack-it-out policy, and placed a cap on the number of people allowed on the trail network at any one time. Just as important, a major environmental education program is underway for the porters who work along the trail.

These are positive steps for the sanctuary, but some people who depend on tourism income are unhappy with the threat that a limit on the number of trail users might pose to them, so the regulations are contentious. Enforcement of "pack it out" rules for every trekker and porter may also be difficult, as sanctuary staff are heavily outnumbered by visitors and are already having trouble enforcing regulations forbidding camping at archaeological sites.

While I walked down from Dead Woman's Pass on that summer day in July, the sun dropped behind a distant Andean peak and light faded from the valley. A fine mist rolled towards the pass from the darkening forests below. All of the tourists had gone. In deepening silence, the route to Machu Picchu, more than just a tourist attraction, seemed a long-lost piece of another world.

In today's world, economic realities may force Peru to encourage the growth of tourism in the Machu Picchu Historical Sanctuary, but more tourism need not cause more damage. We hikers don't need to leave trash, soil erosion, and scorched forests in our wake.

12

Pharmaceutical Companies Can Preserve Rain Forests by Harvesting Medicinal Plants

Lidia Wasowicz

Lidia Wasowicz is a senior science writer for United Press International.

Rain forests contain a greater variety of plant species than any other habitat. Some of these plants, researchers believe, may have valuable medicinal properties that could save the lives of people suffering from diseases such as cancer and AIDS. A research team of Americans and Panamanians has developed a plan to seek out potential pharmaceuticals and promote conservation of rain forests. According to their plan, drug companies would work with developing nations to research plants that could be made into medicines, creating enormous revenues for these cash-starved countries. The researchers believe that developing nations will try to preserve their rain forests if drug research brings in more profits than do the logging and ranching operations that are now destroying the forests.

In the end, the destiny of the world's dwindling rainforests may depend on drugs, diversity and dividends, conclude researchers who spent five years determining the pragmatics of pinpointing plants with pharmaceutical potential beneath the lush canopy of the Panamanian jungle.

In completing their $3-million survey, the investigators have devised what they see as a practical plan to protect nature's delicate handiwork from decimation. Given proper financial incentives, drug companies can work hand-in-hand with developing nations poor in economy but rich in biodiversity to salvage one of Earth's most valuable, and most threatened, natural resources, the international team of scientists maintains.

Their vision hinges the gateway to success on the pharmaceutical industry establishing scientific laboratories in the Third World and hiring local researchers to extract new medicines from plants that, over the eons, have devised defense mechanisms against insects.

> *We have developed a novel approach that provides a direct link between looking for drugs and promoting conservation and economic development in biodiversity-rich countries.*

"Until now, efforts to find drugs in the rainforest haven't really led to rainforest conservation," said Tom Kursar, an associate professor and one of the duo of University of Utah biologists who led the collaborative effort, which included 15 U.S. and Panamanian specialists. "But we have developed a novel approach that provides a direct link between looking for drugs and promoting conservation and economic development in biodiversity-rich countries."

Their own experience bespeaks the soundness of their proposal, the scientists state.

"In our research, not only are we finding potential pharmaceuticals, but we are (also) contributing to conservation of the forests," said Phyllis Coley, a biology professor and Kursar's personal and professional partner.

Searching for drugs in the rapidly vanishing rainforests of developing countries might forestall the disappearance of natural treasures that could fill humanity's coffers, she noted.

"(Rainforests) are home to more species of organisms than any other habitat," Coley told United Press International [UPI]. "The repercussions of losing these habitats are enormous, not only for the species that are lost, but also for global climate, for the livelihood of people living in the tropics and for the goods and services we receive."

A High-Risk, Expensive Process

The so-called bioprospecting route to rainforest salvation is built on the premise that developing nations will work to preserve their wilderness if nondestructive industries—among them drug research, ecotourism and watershed protection—outperform logging and ranching in financial benefits.

The fly in this potential ointment for the ailing economies and disappearing forests of the Third World has been the failure to produce timely, lucrative results. Only a small fraction of compounds derived from plant extracts—in 10,000 or 1 in 5,000, by some rough estimates—actually are developed into drugs. Even when they are, it takes years for the rainforests' home country to start earning royalties.

"The challenge, therefore, is to provide immediate and guaranteed benefits even if royalties are not forthcoming," the biologists note in *Frontiers in Ecology and the Environment*, a journal published by the Ecological Society of America.

Up to one-third of the research carried out by drug companies—which invest $27 billion to $43 billion worldwide each year in such endeavors—could be conducted in the Third World, the researchers estimate.

However, those in the business may have other ideas, a spokesman for the Pharmaceutical Research and Manufacturers of America [PhRMA] suggested.

> *Only a small fraction of compounds derived from plant extracts . . . actually are developed into drugs.*

"Most companies already have more targets in their research bins than they can handle," said Mark Grayson, PhRMA's deputy vice president for communications. The group represents 34 of the biggest names in an industry that invested more than $30 billion in 2002 in discovering and developing treatments and cures.

"As the National Institutes of Health [NIH] points out, only

5 percent of research targets are developed, so there's no shortage of targets," Grayson said in a telephone interview. Looking for medicines in plants growing in developing countries "is nowhere near the top of our priority list," he added.

Grayson noted drug discovery and development is an arduous, high-risk and expensive proposition, and called it "suicide" for a company to establish research projects in areas with small potential for investment recovery or profit making.

Home-Grown Talent

Nevertheless, proponents do not regard the plan as such a hard sell.

"The advantage of the Panama model is that we are not asking for new funds, simply suggesting that it might be productive to invest current funds in new places," Kursar told UPI, "and, in fact, those research dollars might stretch farther in developing nations."

In a mere five years, for example, the pilot project realized:
• the establishment of six laboratories in Panama;
• the employment of home-grown talent, including 10 senior scientists; 57 paid research assistants and 12 student volunteers, and
• the higher education of dozens of local students, with 20 earning bachelors degrees, 12 receiving or working on master's degrees and one embarking on doctoral studies.

"We don't think there is actual resistance to the idea of collaborating with scientists from developing nations, so if we can make it easy for pharmaceutical companies or granting agencies, we think it will actually happen," Kursar said.

The impetus must come from institutions such as the National Institutes of Health, the National Science Foundation, the European Union, non-governmental organizations, conservation groups, the United Nations and non-profit foundations, researchers told UPI. Already, there is some progressive movement afoot, they noted.

For example, the International Cooperative Biodiversity Groups program, conceived in 1991 by the NIH, NSF [National Science Foundation] and the U.S. Agency for International Development to focus on the interrelationship among drug development, biological diversity and economic growth, has just entered its third round of funding projects.

"In part because of the success of the Panama model, (the

ICBG) made it a requirement to have a significant portion of the project based in the (plant) source countries," Kursar said.

Medicine from the Forest

About half of all new drugs come from natural products derived from plants, microbes and, to some extent, animals such as corals and other marine lifeforms, poison arrow frogs and insects, the ICBG notes.

Of the 868 treatments developed between 1981 and 2002, 55 percent had such beginnings, David Newman, Gordon Cragg and Kenneth Snader, all of the National Cancer Institute in Bethesda, Md., noted in an analysis published in the July [2003] issue of the *Journal of Natural Products*. From 2000 to 2002, they traced 50 of 83 new drugs—or 60 percent—to similarly natural roots.

"To stay competitive, companies must find unstudied organisms that may provide novel medicines, the tropics being a very attractive target," Coley said.

> *About half of all new drugs come from natural products derived from plants, microbes and, to some extent, animals such as corals and other marine lifeforms, poison arrow frogs and insects.*

As a bonus, the Panama project yielded the first test of a compound's effect on malaria—a plague that kills a child somewhere in the world every 20 seconds—that does not require radioactivity, thereby making its use plausible in developing countries. Already, scientists from Madagascar have arrived in Panama, eager to learn the technique.

In addition, the Smithsonian Tropical Research Institute in Balboa, Panama—where Coley and Kursar also hold appointments—and Panamanian scientists have obtained a provisional patent for four alkaloid chemicals extracted from local plants.

Laboratory tests by Luis Cubilla Rios of the University of Panama and Luz Romero of Florida State University in Panama revealed the compounds' toxic effect on the parasite that causes leishmaniasis, a disfiguring and potentially fatal disease transmitted by the bite of any of 30 species of sand flies.

Endemic in 88 countries on five continents—Africa, Asia, Europe, North and South America—the infection threatens some 350 million people, according to the World Health Organization. The disease affects an estimated 12 million people worldwide, with 2.4 million new cases and 59,000 deaths reported in 2002 alone.

> *Although drug companies have done little to safeguard this resource, our project agrees that drug discovery could play a key role in saving the rainforest.*

Most often attacking the skin or internal organs, the disease brings on a variety of symptoms, ranging from self-healing but unsightly ulcers to life-threatening infections. Currently, no vaccines or drugs are available to prevent the infection.

Other Breakthroughs

The researchers are establishing mice colonies in Panama to test the safety and effectiveness of the newfound compounds against leishmaniasis. They hope to expand the research to other tropical diseases. Their work—funded by the NIH, NSF and U.S. Department of Agriculture—won praise from Jeffrey McNeeley, chief scientist of the World Conservation Union in Switzerland.

"(The new project) shows how to conduct more of the value-added bioprospecting research in the source country and build the technical capacity of local people while doing so," McNeeley said.

The study brought to light ways to boost the effectiveness of drug discovery by focusing on the chemical arsenal plants have assembled against insects. The scientists tested extracts from leaves carpeting Panama's protected wild lands on breast, lung and nervous system cancer cells; the AIDS virus, and organisms causing malaria, leishmaniasis and Chagas' disease, a parasitic infection with an annual death toll of 50,000. They found younger leaves, not yet toughened in their anti-pest defenses, showed greater chemical activity and higher number of potentially useful compounds than did older ones, even on the same plant.

They also discovered shade-tolerant flora offer a more plentiful source of active substances than the sun worshippers, which can replace insect-ravaged leaves more quickly and, therefore, have less need to develop stronger chemical defenses.

"Probably the most important, from a drug-discovery point of view, is that young leaves are defended by both greater amounts and by unique compounds not found in mature leaves," Coley said. "Thus, conventional collections, which have focused on mature leaves, may have missed much of the chemical promise in plants."

In the next phase, the scientists will work to improve techniques to purify and test promising compounds in mice, continue training Panamanian students and serve as a model for other countries.

"Personally, we have seen the destruction of tropical forests worldwide, and it is very painful," Coley told UPI. "Although drug companies have done little to safeguard this resource, our project agrees that drug discovery could play a key role in saving the rainforest."

13

Buying Shade-Grown Coffee Can Restore Rain Forests

Brian Halweil

Brian Halweil is a research associate at the Worldwatch In-stitute, an organization whose stated mission is to work for an "environmentally sustainable and socially just society."

The selling of coffee has grown into a multibillion-dollar industry in the past decade. The coffee beans fueling this burgeoning business are grown in rain forests. There are two ways to grow coffee: in the shade, which preserves rain forests, and in the sun, which destroys the forest. Coffee beans that are shade grown are raised under the forest canopy. This type of coffee has the best flavor and brings premium prices on the world market. The second type of coffee—the kind most commonly consumed—is grown in the sun where trees have been cut down and the land converted to agricultural fields. In areas in which shade farming has been converted to sun cultivation, the number of plants and animal species has plummeted. The destruction of the rain forest also contributes to global warming and water short-ages. Fortunately, many consumers are willing to pay a bit more for "fair trade" coffee that is certified as shade grown. Not only are they drinking a more flavorful cup of coffee, they are also helping to preserve and restore the rain forest.

Brian Halweil, "Why Your Daily Fix Can Fix More than Your Head: Coffee, If Grown Right, Can Be One of the Rare Human Industries That Actually Restore the Earth's Health," *World Watch*, May/June 2002. Copyright © 2002 by Worldwatch Institute, www.worldwatch.org. Reproduced by permission.

If you are in a coffeeshop—or you've just brewed your own java—you are inhaling microscopic particles of coffee, which carry some of the 800 naturally occurring chemicals that give coffee its seductive aroma. These are the same chemicals, by the way, that can jumpstart your central nervous system—caffeine being the most famous one.

When these molecules enter the nostrils and stimulate the olfactory nerve, it may be hard to think about much more than getting that first swallow. Drinking coffee quickens the heartbeat and makes a person more energetic and alert. Regular coffee drinkers can even experience withdrawal symptoms, if they don't get their fix at the expected time. So if you're starting your day and just want that first cup, it may be hard to muster much interest in where the coffee actually comes from.

But where it comes from has surprising importance for the future of life on a destabilized planet. Coffee is one of those tropical exports that are produced exclusively in the Third World and consumed almost entirely in the First World. (Cocoa, vanilla, and bananas are some other examples.) The beans that are brewed for people in Geneva, Los Angeles, and Tokyo all grow in that waistband of tropical rainforests that girdles the planet between the Tropic of Cancer and the Tropic of Capricorn. At this point, there are basically two ways to grow coffee—in a manner that helps to preserve and restore rainforest, or in a manner that destroys rainforest. And as biologists have stressed, rainforest happens to have disproportionately high value to the Earth's ecological health.

Tropical Deforestation

Until a few decades ago, most of the world's coffee was grown in the understory of rainforests, with farmers looking after the rainforest trees as a natural part of managing their coffee. But now, more and more coffee is produced in what *was* rainforest—clear-cut tracts of land without shade, that give off the dry, burning scent of ammonia fertilizer. Over 40 percent of the coffee area in Colombia, Mexico, Central America, and the Caribbean has been converted to "sun" coffee, with an additional one-quarter of the area in conversion. It's a pattern that is emerging everywhere coffee is grown.

In the short term, this conversion may boost yield because larger numbers of coffee plants can be crowded together in the space where great wild fig trees once stood. But the long-term effect is another story. From an ecological point of view, this conversion is simply another form of tropical deforestation, along with the slash-and-burn clearing by settlers, or the bull-dozing by cattle farmers looking to expand grazing range. When a shade coffee farm is converted to full-sun cultivation, the diversity and number of organisms in the area crashes. The various orchids, mosses, frogs, salamanders, and birds that in-habit a rainforest nearly all need a shady and moist area to build their homes, get food, and survive.

> *There are basically two ways to grow coffee—in a manner that helps to preserve and restore rainforest, or in a manner that destroys rainforest.*

Ornithologists have found that in full-sun plantations, the number of bird species is cut by half, and the number of indi-vidual birds is cut by as much as two-thirds. Most rainforest birds reside in the canopy of trees, rather than on the ground near the coffee plants. The Mot mot, a brilliantly colored bird with a feathered knob at the end of its wire-like tail, which the bird swings from side to side like the pendulum of a clock, lives on berries and insects found in the upper canopies of wild fig, avocado, and coral trees. The insects, in turn, depend on the nectar produced by plants living on the surfaces of these trees—orchids, bromeliads, and cactus. Insect larvae develop in the pools of rainwater captured and stored by these plants, which also happen to be the water source for salamanders, frogs, snakes, and other rainforest animals. But if the highly complex rainforest system is reduced to just a field of coffee shrubs, all these interdependent organisms disappear.

The Benefits of Shade Coffee

According to Jeffrey A. McNeely, Chief Scientist at the World Conservation Union (IUCN). "The widespread conversion to sun coffee is particularly troubling considering that 13 of the world's 25 biodiversity hot spots—those areas that are unusually rich in species and highly threatened—are in coffee country." But what's at stake is not just the inherent worth of the rainforests and the species for which those forests are home. There are also some major benefits for people, both in the places where the coffee is grown *and* in places like the one where you live:

• These rainforests sequester a large share of the world's carbon, and as our atmosphere gets more and more saturated by carbon, that capacity to keep the carbon locked up in plants, and out of our atmosphere, becomes more and more indispensable. When a forest is burned or cut, the carbon is released into the air and becomes a contributor to global warming. Shade coffee helps keep the carbon where it should be.

• The forests—and the shade coffee farms that help preserve them—are essential to the protection of freshwater resources in tropical areas. The vegetative cover and roots of the shade system help to store more water, reducing the incidence of flooding and landslides, and helping to recharge aquifers. Coffee growers in the hillsides surrounding San Salvador, the capital city of El Salvador, are now being encouraged to bring tress back to their farms in order to help the city alleviate its water shortage.

> *When a shade coffee farm is converted to full-sun cultivation, the diversity and number of organisms in the area crashes.*

• Shade coffee requires less pesticide (sometimes none), because undisturbed rainforest is home to birds and insects that devour coffee-plant pests.

• Shade coffee also requires less (or no) chemical fertilizer, because many of the plants that comprise the complex ecosystem of a natural forest add nutrients to the soil. Similarly, the natural system requires less (or no) application of irrigation water, because the greater soil cover and shade reduces water loss through evaporation.

• The biodiversity found in shade coffee farms is a critical asset to people all over the world, because of its potential for developing new medicines, foods, and other resources. The benefits begin with the coffee farmer, who benefits far more from a shade-grown than from a sun-grown crop. On shade coffee farms in Peru, farmers derive nearly 30 percent of their income from sales of firewood, timber, fruits, and medicinal plants found in the shade system—all products which are also consumed by their own households. And these farmers do not have to be constantly working around pesticides.

A Premium Price

Coffee farmers have another incentive, too, to restore the forests on their farms, because when coffee is grown in the shade, it brings a premium price. Coffee companies and drinkers are willing to pay more for beans grown with some consideration for sustaining the forest, which generally means not only creating space for other species but also farming without reliance on toxic agrochemicals. And there are some coffee labels that guarantee growers a minimum price that is generally much higher than the world price. The aid group Oxfam is encouraging Americans and Europeans to seek out and buy this "fair trade" coffee, as "a small but significant way for you to contribute to fighting poverty."

To coffee farmers in Kenya, Colombia, or any other poor country, this premium now means more than ever. Worldwide, the average coffee farmer earns less than $3 a day. For the price we happily pay for a latte, the farmer has to pay for his house, food, clothes, and kids' education. As a result, with commercial coffee prices at their lowest in several decades, many small growers are abandoning their crops. In Mexico, 300,000 coffee farmers have left their farms. When fair trade is practiced, coffee drinkers become involved in improving the lives of distant coffee farmers.

Shade coffee requires less pesticide (sometimes none), because undisturbed rainforest is home to birds and insects that devour coffee-plant pests.

One reason fair trade can pay more is that it offers better *long-term* economics. The coffee farm that resembles an intact forest costs less to maintain. The pesticides and fertilizers that are essential in a plantation setting are expensive substitutes for the free services once provided by the birds, insects, fungus, and other organisms of the forest understory. The coffee plant evolved in the shade of forests in what is now sun-blasted Ethiopia and the Sudan. Remove the forest and you're left with "coffee plants on life support," according to Robert Rice of the Smithsonian Migratory Bird Center. "You've done a number on the soil and the supporting cast of biodiversity," so the plants sooner or later wear out and fall prey to disease.

> *Coffee companies and drinkers are willing to pay more for beans grown with some consideration for sustaining the forest.*

Most of the world's "ethical" coffee—certified as organic, protecting the rainforest, and giving the grower a fair wage—currently comes from Central America and the Caribbean, but the concept can be easily extended to the whole world. The tree and bird species that are protected will vary, as will the languages and cultures of the small farmers that maintain the farms. But the bottom line is that the world's tropical heritage will be preserved.

Reversing Destruction

Exactly how much forest can be preserved? Of the 11.8 million hectares sown to coffee worldwide in 2001, virtually all of it (except the 2.3 million hectares planted in Brazil) is in current or former rainforest. In other words, a global conversion to ethical coffee production would safeguard about nearly 10 million hectares of rainforest. Considering that fires and clear-cuts claim roughly 15 million hectares of rainforest each year, this could be a major move toward actually reversing rainforest destruction. It won't happen immediately, of course. In places where the natural forest has been completely cleared, it would take five to ten years to establish a durable stand of trees. The big question is whether there is enough demand for this "ethical" coffee to keep growers on the land and to encourage them to grow more than just coffee.

At a recent meeting of the International Coffee Organization, major coffee producers and buyers from around the world agreed to limit coffee production in order to boost the world price and help growers around the world stay in business—a move that some analysts think points to a paradigm shift in how coffee companies think about the crop. Ernesto Illy, president of illycaffe, a premium quality coffee company based in Italy, says that the industry understands that coffee drinkers care more and more about the quality of the coffee. "If you want to have beautiful, ripe, and mature, hand-picked cherries [coffee beans], then you have to assure the farmer a decent living," he says. Illycaffe often pays its growers double the world market price to assure such quality.

A "Chicken-and-Egg" Dilemma

In some ways, this presents a "chicken-and-egg" dilemma. On one hand, major coffee companies often argue that even if they wanted to sell shade-grown or fair-trade coffee, there is not enough currently produced and certified to assure a reliable supply. On the other hand, most growers are unlikely to convert until someone shows them the money.

A few major European and American coffee houses, including Starbucks, have now joined the many smaller shops that are offering ethical coffee, certified to be organic, grown in the shade, and/or fairly traded. These shops represent just a small fraction of the market compared with the major buyers worldwide, Procter and Gamble (Folgers), Philip Morris (Maxwell House), and Nestle (Nescafe). In terms of the ethical coffee discussion, the big players—known as "the cans" in industry lingo—haven't even come to the table.

Growing Consumer Concern

Which points to another chicken-and-egg dilemma. Coffee companies are generally unwilling to begin selling shade-grown coffee without some assurance that customers will buy it, and perhaps pay a bit more for it. But there's precedent for thinking that with the help of a reasonable boost from promotion and advertising, a serious shift in demand is possible. With other products, consumer awareness of ethical or environmental implications has brought major changes in the market. Around the world, growing numbers of people are asking questions like, "Am I buying diamonds that financed warlords in Sierra Leone?" "Did kids in a sweatshop stitch together my T-shirt?" "Have these fresh-cut flowers been doused with banned pesticides?"

Humanitarian considerations aside, there may be some

other very good reasons to care how your coffee is grown. "Coffee grown in the shade matures more gradually," says Ernesto Illy, "which makes it more aromatic and gives it a more powerful flavor." Ted Lingle, executive director of the Specialty Coffee Association of America, notes that "organic, shade-grown coffees are beginning to win a disproportionate number of cupping [tasting] competitions around the world."

14

Sustainable Agricultural Practices Are Reversing Deforestation in Costa Rica

Joyce Gregory Wyels

Joyce Gregory Wyels is a California-based travel writer and frequent contributor to Américas *magazine.*

While the rain forest of Costa Rica is a popular destination for tourists, impoverished farmers have cut down more than 80 percent of the forest to practice subsistence farming. In the past decade, however, researchers, environmentalists, and teachers have found a way to reverse the destruction. They are developing educational programs about sustainable agriculture that are increasing ecological awareness while providing financial incentives for farmers to preserve the forest. These programs have improved the prognosis for the rain forest by combatting the problems of soil erosion, wildlife extinction, and global warming caused by deforestation. Costa Rica now has more forest than it did ten years ago. Researchers believe that by increasing knowledge of sustainable agriculture, farming and forests can co-exist for the benefit of all.

Joyce Gregory Wyels, "Common Ground for Farmers and Forests: Alarmed by Signs of Extensive Deforestation over the Past Decades, Groups in Costa Rica are Developing Programs that Combine Ecological Awareness and Sustainable Agriculture," *Américas,* vol. 55, March/April 2003, pp. 22–29. Copyright © 2003 by the Organization of American States. Reproduced by permission of *Américas,* a bimonthly magazine published by the General Secretariat of the Organization of American States in English and Spanish.

With more than 25 percent of its land protected in national parks and private reserves, Costa Rica enjoys an enviable reputation as an ecological paradise. Green-hued travel posters tout cone-shaped volcanoes blanketed by forests, home to a variety of flora and fauna all out of proportion to the diminutive size of this Central American nation. Rare toucans, resplendent quetzals, and scarlet macaws delight bird watchers, while adventure-travel enthusiasts wax lyrical about kayaking mangrove swamps, hiking verdant rain-forest trails, and rafting white-water rivers fringed with tropical foliage. Costa Rica's forests have even spawned a new sport: the ingenious canopy tour, in which participants don rappeling gear to zip through the treetops on cables attached to elevated platforms. From this vantage point, the travel posters have it right: broad vistas of undulating green spread toward the horizon, underscoring the tourism slogan, "All Natural Ingredients."

But a look at the landscape from an even loftier perspective suggests trouble in paradise. NASA (U.S. National Aeronautics and Space Administration) has compiled nearly thirty years' worth of photographs taken from space, which document the tracts of land covered in forest and the growing settlements, farms, and pasturage that continually chew at their edges. In 1993, student interns from EARTH University (Escuela de Agricultura de la Region del Tropico Humedo), with the support of NASA scientists, began interpreting the images. Last summer [2002] the results were released in *Costa Rica desde el espacio* (*Costa Rica from Space*), a compendium of 125 photographs published in book form with bilingual text by NASA and EARTH, with the financial support of UNESCO (United Nations, Educational, Scientific, and Cultural Organization) and Banco San Jose.

> *Whereas forest once covered 99 percent of [Costa Rica], by 1983 it was down to 17 percent.*

The images, which include aerial and field shots as well as photographs from space, cast doubt on Costa Rica's green image. Whereas forest once covered 99 percent of the country, by 1983 it was down to 17 percent. The photographs show traces of fire along both coasts, and great swaths of pastureland re-placing old-growth trees. Forests that once spread from the slopes of the Turrialba Volcano in the Cordillera Central to the flatlands of Tortuguero on the east coast have disappeared.

NASA astronauts, including Costa Rica's own Franklin Chang-Diaz, presented the book at press conferences and other public gatherings last summer. Newspaper editorials warned of dire consequences if the trend continued, one going so far as to predict that if [the capital city] San Jose and the surrounding Central Valley are transformed into a megalopolis, "within twenty-five years we would go from the 'Switzerland of Central America' to the 'Calcutta of the Caribbean'."

Compelling Reasons for Conservation

The loss of forest lands could decimate the carefully nurtured tourism industry, which has surpassed coffee and bananas as Costa Rica's number-one income earner. But reasons for concern go far beyond the loss of tourism revenue. Forest environments prove their worth in more ways than maintaining habitat for ecotourists or even for the wildlife that dwindles as forests become fragmented.

On a global level, tropical rain forests absorb excess atmospheric carbon, thereby reducing global warming. Locally, even the simple act of providing shade helps to regulate temperatures and safeguard organisms that affect plant and animal life all along the food chain. Moreover, trees and their root systems anchor the soil, keeping erosion in check.

One compelling reason for preserving the rain forest stems from our ignorance about the extent of its resources. In Costa Rica, where 0.035 percent of the earth's surface supports 5 percent of the world's biodiversity, the next medical breakthrough or nutritional supplement may be awaiting discovery among the endemic plants and organisms of a little-understood ecosystem.

Some of the most serious damage comes from commercial logging and roads cut into the forest. The heavy equipment that accompanies logging erodes the soil and suffocates streambeds, killing fish and the animals that feed on them. Roads establish new channels for runoff, thereby altering drainage patterns and aggravating erosion.

In Costa Rica, however, forest loss stems less from commercial logging than from people simply clearing land for farms and pasturage as a source of livelihood. "The possibility to own small farms has been something available in Costa Rica for quite a while," says agroecologist Dr. Stephen Gliessman, who has studied farming systems in Costa Rica for the past thirty years. "It's different from other Central American countries in which much less land is available to small farmers."

The Problems of Deforestation

But even when the trees disappear as a result of farmers clearing land for cultivation, the resulting erosion and water contamination contribute to environmental degradation. Especially in the tropics, with its torrential rains, deforestation triggers far-reaching consequences. Agroecologist Dr. Reinhold Muschler cites the cropland on the shoulders of the Irazu Volcano as an example.

"We have very steep hills worked in ways that keep them completely denuded at times," he says. "So the rain washes tons of fertile topsoil away, and it's irreversibly gone. This is one of the main problems linked to deforestation. With the loss of forest cover or a permanent ground cover you have this exposure of the soil, and with that you have tremendous erosion, leaving that landscape denuded and causing problems downstream."

Among the problems caused by deforestation, explains Muschler, are siltation in hydroelectric power plants and in marine coastal areas. In Cahuita National Park, for example, clay particles in the eroded material change the composition of the water. This in turn changes the way the water transmits light, and therefore the coral reef suffers. Says Muschler, "We have seen serious negative effects in many marine environments that are due to deforestation in the hinterlands, sometimes hundreds of kilometers away."

Environmentally Friendly Farming

The good news is that even as rural poverty and the demand for farmland push more people into the forest, concepts of ecology and sustainable agriculture have emerged that promise benefits for both farmers and forests. One group that espouses a holistic approach to conservation and rural development is the Tropical Agricultural Research and Higher Education Center (Centro Agronomico Tropical de Investigacion y Ensenanza—CATIE) on the outskirts of Turrialba.

CATIE grew out of an earlier organization established in

1942 to conduct research and train personnel in tropical agriculture. The center began by building collections of coffee, cocoa, and fruit trees, followed by other crops and forest species. Today the twenty-five-hundred-acre campus contains more than three hundred species of trees and crops, distributed among fields, forests, swamps, and lake. The diversity of its ecological niches attracts some 200 of the 850 bird species in Costa Rica, plus numerous migrant birds.

Another organization that educates scientists regarding conservation issues in tropical regions is the Organization for Tropical Studies (OTS). A consortium of fifty-six universities from the U.S. and Central America operating at three Costa Rican field stations, OTS also embraces a philosophy of reaching out to surrounding communities.

> *With the loss of forest cover or a permanent ground cover you have this exposure of the soil, and with that you have tremendous erosion, leaving that landscape denuded and causing problems downstream.*

But when Stephen Gliessman first studied tropical biology and ecology at OTS as a graduate student in the early 1970s, he encountered a paradox. "I was thinking about how ecology tells us a lot about how nature works," says Gliessman. "I was confounded by the fact that it didn't look to me like agriculture was using the same knowledge. People were clearing forests and farming for a short period of time, then having to abandon their farms and clear more forest. It just didn't seem like that should be happening—there ought to be a way to apply ecology to agriculture so that agriculture could stay permanently on a cleared piece of land and not continually move into the forest to find more after what they cleared had degraded."

After earning his Ph.D., Gliessman went to work for a small private farm in southern Costa Rica, applying his knowledge of ecology to help make Finca Loma Linda work as a sustainable farm and ecosystem. Gliessman presented the results of his research at the First International Congress of Ecology in Tel Aviv, Israel, in 1974. The author of *Agroecology: Ecological Processes in Sustainable Agriculture*, he later organized the agroecology course for OTS and started the Agroecology Program in the Department of Environmental Studies at the University of California Santa Cruz.

Last summer [2002] Gliessman joined Reinhold Muschler of CATIE to coordinate the International Course on Tropical Agroecology and Agroforestry, the first time the course had been offered in Spanish and in Latin America. Twenty-six researchers—agronomists and agroforestry specialists from universities, government agencies, and nongovernmental organizations in twelve countries—came together at the CATIE campus to enhance their knowledge of agroecological principles and to explore ways of helping farmers move toward environmentally friendly farming practices.

Participants in the CATIE course also shared their own innovations, describing coffee-tasting rooms in Matagalpa, Nicaragua, micro-credit programs in Huatusco, Veracruz, Mexico, and a homestay internship program for college students at Costa Rica's Finca Loma Linda that offers learning experiences for both farmers and students.

> *Even as rural poverty and the demand for farmland push more people into the forest, concepts of ecology and sustainable agriculture have emerged that promise benefits for both farmers and forests.*

Juan Jose Jimenez Osorio and Rosana Gutierrez Jimenez, from Yucatan, described a one-year training program in Mani in which young Maya farmers learn about Maya history along with sustainable farming practices. "The school is unique," says Roberta Jaffe, Gliessman's partner and a science educator who applies her skills to supporting sustainable communities. "Young farmers, usually eighteen to twenty-five years old, come from the surrounding pueblos to learn how to enhance their farming practices, and they are taught about basic Maya history." Jaffe expressed surprise that these farmers would need such instruction, inasmuch as they were living the culture. "But," she was told, "most of them don't have an education beyond primary grades. Many of them have never even been to the nearby pyramids."

It was the school in Mani, Escuela de Agricultura Ecologica, that inspired Gliessman and Jaffe to start a networking group from among the researchers present at CATIE last summer. They call it "CAN," for Community Agroecology Network. "These groups were working in isolation," says Jaffe. "We saw that they could benefit tremendously from learning from each other."

A Traditional System

Many of the researchers at CATIE reported that as they spread the gospel of sustainable agriculture, a common response from farmers was, "That's the way my grandparents used to farm." For centuries, indigenous farmers and forest dwellers had intuitively followed sounder ecological principles than the mechanized methods that came into vogue in the 1960s.

According to Muschler, the traditional combination of maize, beans, and squash is an example of crops that complement one another. The beans convert atmospheric nitrogen into a form of nitrogen fertilizer that is useful to the plants and enriches the soil. The corn produces a crop, and once it is harvested the stalks can be used as climbing poles for the beans. The squash provides additional soil cover and produces a nutritious vegetable.

"This is a traditional system that is not a monoculture [in which a single crop is extensively grown]," says Muschler. "This is an intermediate step of polycultures. As you go toward further complicated systems you end up with systems that have annual crops and some perennial crops—like maybe some fruit trees or bushes of different kinds—and ultimately you will have some timber species and maybe other tree species that provide a series of ecological functions."

He lists as examples of those functions microclimate improvement, reduction of wind, and balancing of the water availability in a watershed. That's why there's such a big difference between a forested watershed and a deforested watershed, says Muschler: "It's the presence of the trees and their deep roots that helps sustain the soil and helps the rainwater to infiltrate into the soil and to be retained in the soil." Organic matter from dead leaves and plant roots functions as a sponge in retaining the water. At the same time, certain trees can help to fertilize the crops by converting the nitrogen in the atmosphere to a form that nourishes the plants.

The vaunted "Green Revolution" of the 1960s, however, focused on increasing crop yields without concern for environmental or health problems. Massive applications of chemical fertilizers, herbicides, and pesticides depleted soil fertility and contaminated water, while single crops reduced genetic diversity. Far from today's understanding of "green," the revolution led to an industrial and technological approach to agriculture.

"The Green Revolution with its overemphasis on high yields undermines all of our understanding of applying ecology to agriculture," says Gliessman. "Technology did increase yields, but it created imbalances in other areas. Agroecology gives us a framework for understanding not just the ecology, but how we connect to the health and viability of the communities in which people live."

Solving the Coffee Crisis

Although agroecology applies to crops in general, the topic that kept coming up at CATIE was the global coffee crisis. A glut on the world market has caused a steep drop in prices, so that the grower now earns only 5 percent of the retail market value—or less than production costs. Coffee, an important crop in other Central American economies, is Costa Rica's largest export. One out of four agricultural workers derives a livelihood from coffee growing, and 75 percent come from small farms. "They're at the stage where they're pulling out plants," says Jaffe. Worse yet, some workers and small farmers have been forced off their land and into urban centers.

For those growers affiliated with CATIE, the center has set a minimum fair price paid directly to the farmers, who receive training in farm diversification with native trees, soil conservation, and biological pest and disease management.

As coffee connoisseurs have learned, shade-grown, organic berries produce a better quality coffee than berries exposed to the sun. Several coffee companies that promote shade-grown coffee subscribe to fair-trade practices as well, in which coffee farmers receive a fair share of profits regardless of world price fluctuations. The problem is that so far, in the United States, only two-tenths of 1 percent (0.2 percent) of the coffee sold is fair-trade coffee.

The solution, some believe, lies in paying farmers for the environmental services they provide. Muschler offers the example of members of a village at the bottom of a hill paying fees for the drinking water and irrigation water that's dependent on the watershed farther uphill. Payment would go to those farmers who maintain their land intact in such a way that it can provide the hydrological services of a forest.

Muschler wants to make every consumer of water aware that water comes ultimately from a spring. In addition, everybody who turns on a television should understand that "hydroelectric power (in Costa Rica we have 90 percent of electricity from hydropower) can only function as long as the dam is intact and the lake that feeds the turbine is not subject to siltation from all the soil that is eroded on the hillsides around it."

"We're talking about forest structure and the services a forest can provide in terms of protecting the soil, producing water, tying up carbon dioxide, and protecting biodiversity," says Gliessman. "The bosque de cafe [coffee forest] can do a lot of things a forest does, yet provide a livelihood for the farmers who manage it. When farmers sell their coffee they ought to be able to get a different price based on coffee from a system that protects natural resources, keeps people on the land, reduces the need to cut down any more forest, and maybe even opens up those forests for a certain degree of reforestation."

That's precisely the idea behind a program started two years ago [2000] at Finca Loma Linda. Speaking for the farmers in four cooperatives that have banded together as Programa Pueblos, Darryl Cole-Christensen, who owns Loma Linda, puts it this way: "Treat us fairly in your purchase of our coffee, and we will manage more competently your environment and ours." But despite the high quality of their coffee, the farmers of Programa Pueblos are struggling economically.

The missing link, says Cole-Christensen, is a marketing organization in the U.S. Programa Pueblos has enlisted former student interns to help with direct marketing, as well as faculty, family members, and friends. "From month to month the number of people involved in this marketing structure is increasing," says Cole-Christensen.

Benefiting Consumers and Producers

Jaffe sees CAN, too, as a way of cutting out some of the middle-man profits and "taking back the concept of global village—where global village has been co-opted by multinational businesses—but maybe we can make global village a way of connecting consumer and producer to the benefit of both."

Programa Pueblos is currently building a community center where interns work with families on community and environmental policy. The interns have launched a market study to enable farm families to earn income through diversified, small-scale produce production. They plan to welcome visitors to demonstration plots to showcase pilot research projects that can later be extended to co-op members' farms. Cole-Christensen envisions creating links between producers and consumers by way of a network of e-mail communication and video and multimedia. The hope is to extend "reforestation of our watersheds and the high summits of our mountains to an entire region of Costa Rica." Ultimately, says Cole-Christensen, "we are creating a model that demonstrates how lesser developed areas of the world can achieve economic stability and well-being while also maintaining environmental integrity."

Even now, Muschler sees reason for optimism: "While some ten or fifteen years ago the prognosis for the forest cover of Costa Rica was rather negative and there was a series of satellite images and aerial photographs showing rampant deforestation, over the past five or six years there has been a lot of effort to reforest. I think we are through that trough of deforestation. We have seen a reverse trend, and now Costa Rica has more forest cover than ten years ago."

Organizations to Contact

Bushmeat Crisis Task Force (BCTF)
1700 Connecticut Ave. NW, Suite 403, Washington, DC 20009
(301) 705-6028 • fax: (202) 588-1069
e-mail: info@bushmeat.org • Web site: www.bushmeat.org

The Bushmeat Crisis Task Force, founded in 1999, is a consortium of conservation organizations and scientists dedicated to the conservation of wildlife populations threatened by commercial hunting of wildlife for sale as meat. The primary goals of the BCTF are to focus attention on the bush-meat crisis in Africa, establish mechanisms for information sharing regarding the bush-meat issue, and to facilitate engagement of African partners and stakeholders in addressing the bush-meat issue. The organization publishes the *Bushmeat Bulletin,* fact sheets, research documents, and information packets available on its Web site.

Center for International Forest Research (CIFOR)
PO Box 6596, JKPWB, Jakarta 10065 Indonesia
62-251-622-622 • fax: 62-251-622-100
e-mail: cifor@cgiar.org • Web site: www.cifor.cgiar.org

The Center for International Forest Research is an international research institution committed to conserving forests and improving the livelihoods of people in the tropics. CIFOR's research helps local communities and small farmers gain their rightful share of forest resources, while increasing the production and value of forest products. The center publishes books, journal articles, working papers, reports, and posters.

Committee for a Constructive Tomorrow (CFACT)
PO Box 657224, Washington, DC 20035
(202) 429-2737
e-mail: info@cfact.org • Web site: www.cfact.org

The Committee for a Constructive Tomorrow is a conservative public policy organization focusing on issues of environment and development. CFACT's mission is to enhance the fruitfulness of the earth and all of its inhabitants. The organization does this by pursuing strategies to help meet the basic needs of people around the world, including food, water, energy, and essential human services; promote wise stewardship of wildlife, habitats, and endangered species; and promote safe, affordable technologies and economic policies that reduce pollution and waste and maximize the use of resources. The organization publishes the e-mail newsletter *E-Fact Report* and has links to numerous articles on its Web site concerning topics such as eco-education, energy production, regulations, and land use. Links are also available to one-minute radio commentaries produced by the organization.

Competitive Enterprise Institute (CEI)
1001 Connecticut Ave. NW, Suite 1250, Washington, DC 20036
(202) 331-1010 • fax: (202) 331-0640
e-mail: info@cei.org • Web site: www.cei.org

The Competitive Enterprise Institute encourages the use of private incentives and property rights to protect the environment. It advocates removing governmental barriers in order to establish a system in which the private sector would be responsible for the environment. CEI publications include the monthly newsletter *CEI Update*, the book *The True State of the Planet*, and the report *The World's Forests: Conflicting Signals*.

Environmental Defense Fund
257 Park Ave. South, New York, NY 10010
(212) 505-2100 • fax: (212) 505-0892
Web site: www.edf.org

The fund is a public interest organization of lawyers, scientists, and economists dedicated to the protection and improvement of environmental quality and public health. It publishes the bimonthly *EDF Letter* and the reports *Fires in the Amazon* and *Murder, Mahogany, and Mayhem: The Tropical Timber Trade*.

Global Warming International Center
22W381 Seventy-fifth St., Naperville, IL 60565-9245
(630) 910-1551 • fax: (630) 910-1561
e-mail: syshen@megsinet.net • Web site: www.globalwarming.net

The Global Warming International Center is an international body that disseminates information concerning global warming science and policy. It serves both governmental and nongovernmental organizations as well as industries in more than one hundred countries. The center sponsors research on global warming and its mitigation. It publishes the quarterly newsletter *World Resource Review*.

Greenpeace USA
1436 U St. NW, Washington, DC 20009
(202) 462-1177 • fax: (202) 462-4507
Web site: www.greenpeaceusa.org

Affiliated with Greenpeace International, this organization consists of conservationists who believe that verbal protests against environmental threats are inadequate, and they instead advocate action through nonviolent confrontation. Greenpeace's many concerns include preserving biodiversity and preventing pollution. It publishes *Greenpeace Magazine* as well as books and reports, including *Principles and Guidelines for Ecologically Responsible Forest Use*.

Heritage Foundation
214 Massachusetts Ave. NE, Washington, DC 20002-4999
(202) 546-4400 • fax: (202) 546-8328
Web site: www.heritage.org

The Heritage Foundation is a conservative think tank that supports free enterprise and limited government in environmental matters. Its publications, such as the quarterly magazine *Policy Review* and the occasional papers "Heritage Talking Points," include studies on environmental regulations and government policies.

Rainforest Alliance
665 Broadway, Suite 500, New York, NY 10012
(888) 693-2784
e-mail: canopy@ra.org • Web site: www.rainforestalliance.org

The mission of the Rainforest Alliance is to protect ecosystems and the people and wildlife that depend on them by transforming land use practices, business practices, and consumer behavior. Companies, cooperatives, and landowners that participate in the alliance's programs meet rigorous standards that conserve biodiversity and provide sustainable livelihoods. The Rainforest Alliance is collaborating with farmers, workers, business leaders, NGOs, governments, scientists, and local communities in over fifty countries around the world to develop and implement standards that are socially and environmentally responsible as well as economically viable. Rainforest Alliance publications include: *The Canopy*, a quarterly publication for Rainforest Alliance members; *Eco-Exchange*, a bimonthly publication that goes to two thousand journalists, conservationists, scientists, and government agencies; *Rainforest Matters*, a brief publication that provides conservation news, program developments, original poetry, interviews, and species profiles; *Eco-Education Matters*, a monthly e-mail newsletter; *Sustainable Market Update*, the latest news from the Certified Sustainable Products Alliance; and "RA Perspectives;" publications; interviews; and opinion papers from its staff experts.

World Resources Institute
1709 New York Ave. NW, Washington, DC 20006
(202) 638-6300 • fax: (202) 638-0036
e-mail: lauralee@wri.org • Web site: www.wri.org

The World Resources Institute conducts policy research on global resources and environmental conditions. It publishes books, reports, and papers; holds briefings, seminars, and conferences; and provides the print and broadcast media with new perspectives and background materials on environmental issues. The institute published the books *The Right Climate for Carbon Taxes: Creating Economic Incentives to Protect the Atmosphere* and *The Greenhouse Trap: What We're Doing to the Atmosphere and How We Can Slow Global Warming*.

Worldwatch Institute
1776 Massachusetts Ave. NW, Washington, DC 20036-1904
(202) 452-1999 • fax: (202) 296-7365
e-mail: worldwatch@worldwatch.org • Web site: www.worldwatch.org

Worldwatch is a research organization that analyzes and focuses attention on global problems, including environmental concerns such as maintaining biodiversity and the relationship between trade and the environment. It compiles the annual *State of the World* anthology and publishes the bimonthly magazine *World Watch* and the Worldwatch Papers series, which includes *Saving the Forest: What Will It Take?* and *Reforesting the Earth*.

Bibliography

Books

Rosita Arvigo
Rainforest Home Remedies: The Maya Way to Heal Your Body and Replenish Your Soul. San Francisco: HarperSanFrancisco, 2001.

Bruce Braun
The Intemperate Rainforest: Nature, Culture, and Power on Canada's West Coast. Minneapolis: University of Minnesota Press, 2002.

Catarina Cardoso
Extractive Reserves in Brazilian Amazonia: Local Resource Management and the Global Political Economy. Burlington, VT: Ashgate, 2002.

David Cleary
The Brazilian Rainforest: Politics, Finance, Mining and the Environment. London: Economist Intelligence Unit, 1991.

Wade Davis
Penan: Voice for the Borneo Rainforest. Vancouver: Western Canada Wilderness Committee—Wild Campaign, 1990.

Robert A. Fimbel, Alejandro Grajal, and John G. Robinson, eds.
The Cutting Edge: Conserving Wildlife in Logged Tropical Forest. New York: Columbia University Press, 2001.

Fred P. Gale
The Tropical Timber Trade Regime. New York: St. Martin's, 1998.

Ricardo A. Godoy
Indians, Markets, and Rainforests: Theory, Methods, Analysis. New York: Columbia University Press, 2001.

Marc Herman
Searching for El Dorado: A Journey into the South American Rainforest on the Trail of the World's Largest Gold Rush. New York: Doubleday, 2003.

Bruce M. Knauft
Exchanging the Past: A Rainforest World of Before and After. London: University of Chicago Press, 2002.

Ian McAllister and Karen McAllister
The Great Bear Rainforest: Canada's Forgotten Coast. San Francisco: Sierra Club, 1997.

Premilla Mohanlall
Green Malaysia: Rainforest Encounters. Kuala Lumpur, Malaysia: Malaysian Timber Council, 2002.

Arnold Newman
Tropical Rainforest: Our Most Valuable and Endangered Habitat with a Blueprint for Its Survival into the Third Millennium. New York: Checkmark, 2002.

Sara Oldfield
Rainforest. Cambridge, MA: MIT Press, 2002.

116

Susan E. Place, ed.	*Tropical Rainforests: Latin American Nature and Society in Transition.* Wilmington, DE: Scholarly Resources, 1993.
Richard B. Primack, ed.	*Timber, Tourists, and Temples: Conservation and Development in the Maya Forest of Belize, Guatemala, and Mexico.* Washington, DC: Island, 1998.
Andrew Revkin	*The Burning Season: The Murder of Chico Mendes and the Fight for the Amazon Rain Forest.* Washington, DC: Island, 2004.
Charles Russell	*Spirit Bear: Encounters with the White Bear of the Western Rainforest.* Toronto: Key Porter, 2002.
Candace Slater, ed.	*In Search of the Rain Forest.* Durham, NC: Duke University Press, 2003.
Marie-Claude Smouts	*Tropical Forests, International Jungle: The Underside of Global Ecopolitics.* New York: Palgrave Macmillan, 2003.
Philip Stott	*Tropical Rainforests: Political and Hegemonic Myth-Making.* London: Institute of Economic Affairs, 1999.
Sven Wunder	*Oil Wealth and the Fate of the Forest: A Comparative Study of Eight Tropical Countries.* New York: Routledge, 2003.

Periodicals

Simon Birch	"Saving a Spiritual Home: The Success of the Campaign to Save Canada's Great Bear Rainforest Is Being Heralded as a Model Solution for Conserving the World's Remaining Ancient Forests," *Geographical*, April 2002.
Andrew Brackenbury	"Liberian Logs Fuel War: In Liberia, the Plunder of the Rainforest Has Taken On a New, Sinister Twist—It's Paying for Bloody Warfare, Facilitating Arms Trafficking and Propping Up One of Africa's Most Corrupt Regimes. Meanwhile the International Timber Industry Continues to Profit from These 'Logs of War,'" *Geographical*, August 2002.
Mark L. Clifford, Hiroko Tashiro, and Anand Natarajan	"The Race to Save a Rainforest; Can an Experiment in Indonesia Prove the Merits of Sustainable Logging to Big Timber?" *Business Week*, November 24, 2003.
Julie Cohen	"Flying Colours: The Rainforest of Trinidad and Tobago Are an Ornithologist's Dream," *Geographical*, May 2002.
Steve Davidson	"Rainforest More or Less? Steve Davidson Considers How Tropical Forests Might Shape Up in a Warmer World," *Ecos*, April/June 2002.

Barbara J. Fraser	"Joining Forces for Peru's Rainforest," *NACLA Report on the Americas*, May/June 2003.
George Furukawa	"The Mother of the Rainforest: Careful Restoration Is Bringing Koa Trees, Native Birds and Authenticity Back to a Hawaiian Rainforest," *American Forests*, Winter 2002.
Karen Ann Gajewski	"Illegal Logging of 280,000 Kilometers of the Amazon Rainforest," *Humanist*, January/February 2003.
Darren Guyaz	"Saving Chile's 'Redwoods': A New Direction for the Valdivian Rainforest," *Earth Island Journal*, Summer 2004.
Margot Hornblower	"Next Stop, Home Depot: With a Record of Converting the Corporate, the Rainforest Action Network Eyes Its Biggest Quarry," *Time*, October 19, 1998.
Gary Graham Hughes	"Smelter Threatens Chilean Landscape: Megaproject Moves Forward Despite Widespread Opposition: Dams Will Drown over 25,000 Acres of Temperate Rainforest and Riparian Habitat, Roads Will Increase Siltation, a Million Tons of Minerals Will Be Trucked In, and 600,000 Tons of Waste Left Behind," *Earth Island Journal*, Spring 2003.
Katherine Kerin	"A New Profit Motive: The Bottom Line Is Preserving the Environment," *E*, January/February 2002.
Charles C. Mann	"The Real Dirt on Rainforest Fertility: Ancient Amazonians Left Behind Widespread Deposits of Rich, Dark Soil, Say Archaeologists. Reviving Their Techniques Could Help Today's Rainforest Farmers Better Manage Their Land," *Science*, August 9, 2002.
Aaron Midler	"Taste the Rainforest," *E*, September/October 2004.
June Nash	"Indigenous Development Alternatives," *Urban Anthropology and Studies of Cultural Systems and World Economic Development*, Spring 2003.
Fred Pearce	"A Mirror to Cool the World: If the Gulf Stream Fails and the Rainforest Disappears, Would a Quick Fix Buy Enough Time for the World to Overcome Its Apathy and Do Something About Global Warming?" *New Scientist*, March 27, 2004.
Phill Pullinger	"Loggers on the Prowl: Largely Unknown to Most of the World, the Tarkine in Tasmania Is Australia's Largest Tract of Ancient, Untouched Rainforest. It Doesn't Even Feature on the Tourism Maps but It Is Uppermost in the Minds of Forestry Tasmania," *Habitat Australia*, June 2003.
Paul Roscoe and Borut Telban	"The People of the Lower Arafundi: Tropical Foragers of the New Guinea Rainforest," *Ethnology*, Spring 2004.

Erik Stokstad	"Too Much Crunching on Rainforest Nuts?" *Science*, December 19, 2003.
Philip Stott	"Jungles of the Mind: The Invention of the Tropical Rain Forest," *History Today*, May 2001.
Lee Tan	"War of the Wood: The Battle to Save Asia Pacific's Largest Stand of Untouched Rainforest Is a Risky Business, According to ACF Asia Pacific Coordinator Lee Tan," *Habitat Australia*, December 2004.
U.S. Newswire	"Land Deal Opens Door to Protecting 147,500 Acres of Chilean Rainforest," November 11, 2003.
Thomas H. White Jr. and Fernando Nunez-Garcia	"From Cage to Rainforest," *Endangered Species Bulletin*, July/December 2003.
S.J. Willott, D.C. Lim, S.G. Compton, and S.L. Sutton	"Effects of Selective Logging on the Butterflies of a Bornean Rainforest," *Conservation Biology*, August 2000.

Index

122